I Never Wanted a Dog

Stacie Sauber

Unless otherwise marked, Scripture quotations are taken from the *New King James Version*® (NKJV). Copyright © 1982 by Thomas Nelson. Used by permission. All rights reserved.

Cover photo by David C. Ball
Designballs Creative, and fellow dog lover

Heart & Paw print image courtesy of:
https://www.clipartkey.com

Lyrics to "Reckless Love" by Cory Asbury, Caleb Culver, Ran Jackson, Bethel Music Publishing, Be Essential Songs, and Watershed Music Group

Lyrics to "Jesus Loves the Little Children," public domain.

www.BurkhartBooks.com

Bedford, Texas

Dedication

To my four children:
Natalie, Sydney, Felice, and Mylon Johnson.
I hope this book helps make more real to you the never-ending love,
patience, kindness, and compassion of God.

Acknowledgments

Thanks to my husband, Randy Wolf, for his immeasurable support throughout this quest for Clovis. With your encouragement, help, and understanding, I was able to spend the time needed to win her over.

Thanks to the friends and neighbors who so willingly gave food, treats, blankets, and even a dog bed to help with this endeavor.

Special thanks to Robby and Paula Ritchey and Tim and Julie Lamont, who not only provided food and water for Clovis but, along with Jimmy and Nety Idoski, allowed me to spend countless hours on or near their properties, befriending Clovis.

Thanks to ALL who prayed for Clovis—my Bible study ladies, Pat, Jerry, and your crews of men, friends Rick and Terry, and our hometown neighbors in Southlake and Grapevine who watched and prayed for Clovis' safe capture.

A big heartfelt thanks to The Vet Gals and Guys, who were able to come to the house to give Clovis her vet's first appointments when she wasn't ready to get in a car and travel yet.

Thank you, friend, neighbor, and veterinarian Beverly Unger-Zipfel, who helped us through Clovis' heartworm treatments, along with her support and encouragement.

Thank you, Marvin Cloud, who coached me through the writing process, helping me to be able to write and finish this book.

Thank you to Tim Taylor of Burkhart Books, who saw this project through to the end, enabling me to get Clovis' story into the hands of readers.

Lastly, thanks to all of you who encouraged me to write this book. Some of you I know personally, while others only from *Nextdoor*. Your interest in Clovis' story drove me to pursue this venture.

Contents

Dedication

Acknowledgments

Introduction IX

Chapter 1 11

Chapter 2 21

Chapter 3 33

Chapter 4 43

Chapter 5 51

Chapter 6 59

Chapter 7 71

Chapter 8 77

Photo Gallery 85

Chapter 9 105

Chapter 10 111

Chapter 11 119

Chapter 12 127

Chapter 13 135

Chapter 14 143

Chapter 15 153

Chapter 16 167

Epilogue 177

About the Author

Introduction

When I first began this mission of helping a poor stray dog, I had no idea how my life would be so turned upside-down. What I thought would take a couple of weeks, maybe a month, turned into almost an entire year of my life.

Never could I have imagined that a lonely, almost wild-like dog would touch me the way she did. I am convinced that had I been able to capture her in a quick and timely manner, I would still be the same person I was before. But no, God had other plans.

During this 10-month-long ordeal, I was taught patience, compassion, and never-ending love, but what I was learning about myself and how God sees me was being reinforced as I strove to win Clovis' heart.

In the same ways I was wooing Clovis—the ways I was providing for her and taking care of her—God was doing the same for me. He wants to do the same for you.

The lessons I learned from this journey are probably far too vast and intimate for me to convey. Since I am not a writer by profession, this book is by no means an attempt at a "great literary piece." It is, however, my attempt to simply tell my story. This is the story of how a sweet but lonely and scared stray dog of three years helped change my life and how I changed hers.

I only hope you will understand just how much God loves and cares for you as well.

Stacie Sauber

Chapter 1

*"To everything there is a season,
a time for every purpose under heaven ..."*

Ecclesiastes 3:1

I never wanted a dog. Not because I don't like them, but because my life just couldn't afford the attention and finances a dog would need. I was a divorced mother of four children, ages three to ten, and my life was full enough. For fifteen years, it was full of working to provide. Full of homework. Full of driving kids to soccer, basketball, track, and band. Just plain full. I couldn't fathom how in the world I could fit a dog into our home. If I was going to be a dog mom, I wanted to be a good one. I was just too overwhelmed with raising four children, let alone trying to care for another being that needed a lot of attention.

Enter cats. Cats were easy. They don't need walking or letting out to do their business. They sleep a lot but still cuddle with you—at least when they want to. They can even be left alone for a day or two if you're out of town, with just a neighborhood kid coming by to check on their food and water. Not so with a dog. It just wasn't the right time.

As the children grew up, we had several cats, and we loved them all dearly. We still have two—Rocky, a huge part Maine Coon cat, and Thomas, an orange tabby. Cats were all I ever really wanted because, as I said, I NEEDED EASY.

I have a good friend, Mindi Evans-Lombe, whom I have known for at least a decade. Mindi and I met through running, and our friendship was formed through running. We would meet early in the morning before we started our hectic days to run and chat about our lives. Mindi, an elementary school PE teacher, and I hit it off as friends almost immediately.

Our love of running was at the top of our favorites "to do" list, and our sense of humor was flat-out made for each other! We just clicked as friends. Mindi has no human children; she has dogs. Plural. She usually has two to five dogs of her own and fosters dogs as well. She is a dog lover and so wanted me to be one too. She was always trying to get me to adopt one of her fosters. "Come on, Stacie, I think you need a dog!" My response? "I'll adopt a dog when you have a baby." And I was serious. I completely understand that many people look at their dogs as their children. I look at my kitties as part of the family. But pets are not the same as having children. I don't have to do homework with my pets. I don't have to keep them off drugs or keep them from getting pregnant. I don't have to worry about what kind of human being they will grow up to be, how I will pay for college or how they will support themselves, or who they might marry. I certainly can't kennel them when I want to go out for the night with my friends. That is why we have had cats for 20 years and counting.

Before I begin telling you how we came to have our new member of the family, I need to bring you from 2000 to 2014. After having been single again for almost 15 years, kids now all grown up, and life settling down somewhat, I happened to meet him. One day, while starting before dawn for my long Sunday morning run, I entered our running club's clubhouse to find a man I had never met before. Being a member of the Lake Grapevine Runners and Walkers was the only thing in my life in those 15 years that helped keep me sane other than my faith. I joined to have a few running buddies and ended up with lifelong friends.

Every weekend for several years, I would run from the clubhouse, in Grapevine, TX, with my friends, chatting, laughing, and just having a great time while getting in my much-loved run. Grapevine is located in a unique area of North Texas. To the southeast, about 25 miles, lies Dallas. To the southwest, about 25 miles, lies Fort Worth. Grapevine Lake borders the city of Grapevine to the north and provides a beautiful place to boat, kayak, and run. The city itself is not very large at about 55,000 residents, and still has that hometown feel, even though the Dallas Ft Worth International airport is only a few minutes away. The town is surrounded by a metroplex of about 6.5 million people. For a busy metropolitan area, Grapevine provides a much-needed escape from the hustle and bustle of everyday life.

Our running clubhouse was just a stone's throw away from the lake in an old rundown bait shop that our club rented for our weekly gatherings. Most running clubs around the nation meet in parks or designated areas to go for a run together. The thing that made our club special was the clubhouse. It was small, old, and dirty, but we all loved the clubhouse! It was a place for us to meet on the weekends, head out for a run together near Lake Grapevine, and then hang out afterward, sharing stories. The clubhouse was very basic with just concrete flooring, a tiny bathroom, and one small window. We had tables, chairs, and coffee pots galore, along with a refrigerator for snacks and sports drinks. The décor consisted of race t-shirts that people would hang from the ceiling.

The front had a garage door that rolled open so everyone could gather inside or outside and visit. We even had a picnic table out under the tree in the back. Just down the road, a few hundred yards, was the lake. After our runs, we would see cars, boats, and kayaks heading to the lake. Such a peaceful place to gather. Overall, it was quite a haven for us runners. We held various social events throughout the year for our members, as well as put on races that drew several hundred from the area for a bit of fun and competition. It was just what the doctor ordered for me. I looked forward to my weekend runs, and January of 2014 was no different.

I thought I knew just about everyone in the club. I also thought there was no way on earth I would ever date anyone from the club because, quite honestly, they were my running buds. My sweaty, smelly, early morning running buds. These were the people who saw me at my worst. When you finish a 20-mile run in preparation for a marathon, you never look your best. You never imagine someone might find you appealing! Plus, 95% of the men were married. So, I never gave dating a thought when it came to my running club. It was my escape. And it just wasn't the right time. Until that January.

I walked into the clubhouse that day in January to find a man filling the water jugs that we put out on the course for the runners. We had 4, 5-gallon jugs that we would fill with water and Gatorade. They would then get taken to various places along our running route, along with paper cups, making it quite easy for runners to stop and drink. Our members signed up and took turns with this "water duty" every weekend. Visiting runners would never be expected to have water duty. So, when I saw him, I thought, "who is this guy?" I'd never seen him before, but he couldn't be new because visiting runners would never be putting the water out. At 4:30 in the morning, and dressed for cold winter running, I probably wasn't in my most pristine "meet the man you will marry" outfit. My goodness, I'm sure I didn't even have lip balm on, let alone makeup or hair done!

"Hi, I'm Stacie Sauber. I don't think we have met before!"

"Hi, I'm Randy Wolf. Nice to meet you! You're out early for a run."

Dressed for the cold weather with running tights, a jacket, gloves, and a hat, I couldn't get a very good look at him, but his smile was all I needed.

"Yes, I have a long one today and like to get started early so I can get back home to get ready for church. Thanks for putting the water out!"

"Sure … have a great run."

I couldn't stop thinking about this man. I kept repeating his name over and over in my head so I wouldn't forget it. Something about him seemed so genuine. So sweet. So kind. His smile caught my eye, but his voice is what stuck in my head. With just a few words, I imagined that he was an honest and compassionate man.   Yet I didn't even know if he was married or how old he was, let alone what kind of person he might be.   But that didn't stop me from wondering.

When I got home after that run, I ran to my computer. Thank goodness for Google. Ah, he's 58 years old (I was 50 at that time), so that's good— not too old, not too young. He runs and bikes and has a lot of racing results out there. What else can I find out? He lives near the clubhouse, just two or three blocks away. Yes, I was stalking. About a month went by, and I didn't see him again. I was wondering if I ever would.

One morning in late March, after a run, my dog momma friend, Mindi, and I were walking back to the clubhouse. As we talked about how school was going for her and how many days until spring break, I mentioned that I had met Randy back in January but hadn't seen him since.   Mindi didn't know who he was either, so I told her the only things I had discovered through Google. Then, as if he had heard us talking about him, he came running up from behind us, heading back to the clubhouse. I whispered, "That's him! That's the guy I was telling you about." My pace picked up—I wanted to get back to the clubhouse before he left and continue my investigation. Mindi was more than willing to help with this.

After morning runs, many runners stay and hang out, visiting and enjoying the morning and sipping coffee. Randy was no exception that day. Mindi and I sat down on the concrete porch of the clubhouse close to each other, just visiting, whispering to each other, and trying to get a feel for who this guy was and what he was like. Other runners came along as they finished their morning runs, grabbed plastic chairs from the clubhouse, and formed a circle just in front of the clubhouse porch.

While everyone visited with each other, Mindi and I joked, laughed, and whispered back and forth. We were like two young schoolgirls giggling over the boy on the playground they had a crush on. I later learned that Randy seemed to be very liked among those who knew him and that he was single. Relief. I had no idea what he did for a living, whether he had been married before or if he had children. That's where it ended. I'm going to have to step up my game.

Welcome Easter weekend, 2014. I already had a huge bag of plastic Easter eggs filled with candy that I was going to put out on the trails for all my running friends that Easter morning. A nice surprise for the dedicated group that I knew would be out, even on a holiday. This was also my chance to see Randy. He was signed up for water duty that day, which I had noticed earlier in the week. Using my sleuth skills, I emailed our former club president, Kelly Richards, as I knew she had a member list with contact information for everyone.

"Hey Kelly, can you send me Randy Wolf's contact info? I have a favor to ask of him."

It was that easy. I sent him an email, telling him if he would help me spread the Easter eggs on the trail before the sun came up, I would help him with the water duty.

"I would love to help you play Easter Bunny!" he replied.

DONE. How could it have been that easy? We communicated back and forth about the details, and we were all set for our Easter egg hunt. Easter came, and that was the first morning that we conversed. At a bright and early 5:00 am, I helped him load the coolers of Gatorade into his car and deliver them to their locations, and he then helped me spread the eggs. We carried the large bags of eggs along the concrete bike path and dirt trails, scattering the eggs as we went. I knew after 20 minutes with this man that I wanted to consider him as someone I would like to date. He was so talkative and inquisitive! We talked about so much for such a little time that we were together. Again, I noticed how kind and gentle he seemed to be. He seemed truly interested in me, too, asking me questions about myself, my children, and my running.

After spreading the eggs, we went back to the clubhouse before the majority of the other runners arrived. There was a small group that was there before the official 7:00 am start time, so we decided to head out for a three-mile warm-up run. This was going to be perfect! A chance for me to see him around other people. How would he interact? Is he well-liked by the other club members? We ran slowly that morning, all of us talking the whole time. Still being cautious, I surmised that he was a good man. That's what I wanted—a good man.

So many things popped out at me about his character over the next few weeks. Two things stood out: Number 1, he called his mom almost every day to talk to her. YES! Number 2, he had an elderly lab, Rowdy, that was now blind in one eye and had severe arthritis. Randy would carry Rowdy up the stairs of his house to go to bed with him and carry him back downstairs in the morning to go outside. He took Rowdy everywhere with him. He even told me that he would take him to races with him, go for runs with him, even swim with him! Randy would put Rowdy in an innertube, tie the innertube around his waist, and go swimming in the lake, pulling Rowdy behind him. "Afterwards, I usually go to *Whataburger* and get a burger for me and one for Rowdy, and we sit at the lake and eat." Yes, this was a good man!

Randy and I began dating a short time after our Easter Bunny escapade. We both loved to run, so we would meet at various times to run together. We also would swim together at the lake in the summer at nearby Meadowmere Park or ride our bikes through town. Our dates were easy. Laidback. Enjoyable. Nothing with Randy ever seemed contrived. It just felt right.

Not long after Randy and I began dating, however, my cat, Rocky, began having trouble jumping. At this time, he was only about two years old. The vet appointment did not go well. We found out that because of Rocky's breed and large stature, he was prone to hip dysplasia. He would need surgery. Now, let me tell you that a single mother of four who is struggling just to pay bills does not want to hear that her cat needs hip surgery! I was crying. I had no idea what I would do. The vet was going to give me a discount, but even so, it would be $1500! How would I ever come up with that? Then Randy stepped up. We had only been dating about three weeks when he brought me an envelope with $500. I didn't know what to do! I barely knew this man, yet here he was, giving me money for my cat's surgery.

"I can't accept this, Randy!"

"But I want you to have it. I even asked one of my clients if I should give it to you just to make sure it was OK, and she asked me, 'Would you give money to help someone else who you aren't dating for their pet's surgery?' and I said 'Yes.' So, she said there was nothing wrong with me giving you this money. Please, I want to help. It's for Rocky."

I didn't know what to say. I still wasn't sure what I was going to do for the remainder of the cost, but a few days later, I would come home from work to find that my daughter, Sydney, had sold her drum set that she loved to help pay for Rocky's surgery. She handed me a Mother's Day card, and inside she wrote:

"Happy Mother's Day, Mom! I love you. Here's the rest of the money for Rocky. I didn't want you to worry about it at all. Don't give me any crap about it because you've made so many sacrifices for us; the least I could do is make one for the best mom in the world."

In the envelope was $800! My heart was overjoyed. I'm not sure if the joy was so much because Rocky would have his surgery or Sydney gave it from her heart. I'll never forget that gesture!

Rocky had his surgery and recovered and is still with us today. He still can't jump very well, but he is no longer in pain. Sydney loved Rocky, and she loved me. Randy barely knew me but he had a love for animals. I realized then that Randy's love for animals was finding a way into my heart.

The next several months were filled with getting to know each other better. Because we spent many of our dates either running, biking, or swimming at the lake, we had plenty of time to converse. We weren't watching movies or simply going out to eat. We spent quality time together, doing things we loved, all while having plenty of time for talking. Randy became aware of the many struggles I had as a single mom with four children, and he didn't seem to be frightened by it. I would have certainly understood any man not wanting to take on that responsibility, but Randy didn't seem phased. Randy had no children of his own; however, he had been married before and had step-children that he had helped raise. This made me feel much better about our scenario. I needed a man who understood what it was like to have children, yet I wasn't sure that even I wanted to add more children to my life. Four was difficult. Four was enough. It was as if God had placed the perfect man for me in my life at just the right time.

Roughly a year later, Randy proposed to me, which is somewhat a miracle considering he initially thought Mindi and I were a couple! He had noticed me, but when he saw Mindi and me walking together and then sitting close together whispering and talking, he just assumed she was my girlfriend. Obviously, he found out that was not true, and we married in April of that same year, sold both of our homes, and bought a new house together—a fixer-upper but not far from where both of us had lived before. My youngest son, Mylon, was graduating from high school that spring, so the timing of everything was perfect. I had never wanted to re-marry while my kids were still in school. I needed to focus on them. I dated some, but nothing serious. Randy and I were going to wait until June, after Mylon's high school graduation, to marry, but one day Mylon said to me, "Mom, it's OK! You don't have to wait. Go ahead and get married!" Until that moment, it just wasn't the right time. Until Randy.

Right before we married, we talked about where we would live. Both of our homes were fine, but we thought maybe a new home together would be the best way to go. I didn't want to feel like a visitor in his home, and I certainly didn't want him to feel like that in mine. We would ride bikes on the weekends, just going through neighborhood after neighborhood, looking at homes and places we thought we might be interested in. After we married, Randy sold his house and moved into mine for the time being. At that point, we began actively looking. We knew what area we wanted, but not much was available. I'd like to say we got lucky, but we believe God led us to the house we have now. We were driving down the road one day, about a mile from the home we were living in when a man was putting up a sign in the yard. FOR SALE BY OWNER. We called immediately! It was quite a fixer-upper, and, frankly, most people around this area would have called it a "tear down." Randy didn't seem interested in it at first.

All he could see was the old. The rundown. The tasks that needed to be done. I saw the property. The yard. The location. We both, however, saw the work. So much work. After looking at it a second and third time, we decided to buy it. It would need a lot of repairs and updating, but Randy and I were willing to do as much of it as we could ourselves. Living just a mile down the road from this house made it easier. We could renovate the house while living elsewhere. For four months, we worked at our jobs and worked on the house. That's all we ever did. We joked that if our marriage survived the first year, including renovating a house, we would last forever. It was a lot of work but also a lot of fun.

We did hire people to do some of the work we couldn't do, but some days our workouts that we usually got in at the gym, we got in at home. These "workouts" consisted of scraping popcorn ceilings, ripping out flooring in every room, painting every room and ceiling in the house, and even replacing all the doors and baseboards ourselves. One project would lead to another one. Probably the most physically intensive project we completed was all the flagstone walkways. When we purchased the home, there was virtually no grass. No landscaping. No walkways from the house to the garage or the driveway. Randy and I planned, prepped, and then moved over 5000 pounds of flagstones into their positions. Three times.

We didn't get it just the way we wanted it the first time, so being the perfectionists we are, we decided to do it all over again, and yet again. These flagstone walkways led to the next project. The final project. The gym. Randy and I are both fitness trainers and nutrition coaches. When we first met, I had no idea that he had the same profession as me. When I learned this tidbit, I almost recoiled. It's not an easy profession. Building a client base isn't easy.

People cancel, travel, and some days just flat don't show up. The income is up and down. The schedule is sometimes crammed and other times non-existent. Work hours can be crazy, beginning some days at 5:00 am and not ending until 7:00 pm to accommodate clients' schedules. It can be uneasy. Being self-employed sounds very romantic to some as though you must have it so good! But with no benefits, no insurance, and no sick days, it can be quite stressful. When I heard Randy tell me that he, too, was a fitness trainer, I wasn't sure it would work. When would we ever see each other? Luckily for both of us, our schedules worked out beautifully, and we were able to spend more time together than I had ever imagined. The doubts I had about our professions colliding were soon wiped away. Once again, I'm sure the Lord had His hand in that.

Up until this time, I worked at my studio in Southlake, about 3 miles from my home. Randy worked at The Four Seasons Resort and Club in Las Colinas, about a 20-minute drive from home, for 35 years. Our new home had a detached garage that looked somewhat like a barn. It had the shape of a barn but a garage door on the front, as well as two other entry doors. It was in a perfect spot to turn into a gym. Randy couldn't see it, but I could.

I knew that if we renovated that space, I could close my business and work from home. We worked tirelessly to finish it, and in November of 2015, I began working from home! It was such a wonderful move. We had a new home together, and everything was falling into place. This new "fixer" home was surrounded by 4-5 acres of city property and Corp of Engineers property. We had woods and fields all around our home. Deer in the backyard every day. Several deer. On one occasion, I looked out to find 17 does and bucks surrounding our property.

Occasionally, we would catch sight of a bobcat or fox, and there were coyotes galore. Their creepy, howling barks woke me in the night when our windows were open. We also had visiting wild turkeys throughout the year—sometimes up to 15 of them! They were entertaining to watch as the males spread their feathers and strutted in front of the hens during mating season. We had a show of animals behind our home! In front of our home and across the street was also a two-acre treed plot with just one house on it. Peaceful, calm, serene setting. Seemed like country living, but just around the corner were Grapevine and Southlake.

Between church, running, and work, my whole world took place within about a two-mile radius. It was fantastic! Life was rolling along as expected. Working, cooking, cleaning, exercising, going to church—all the normal activities of life. Then out of the blue, one day, I saw him.

Chapter 2

"And we know that all things work together for good to those who love God, to those who are the called according to His purpose."
Romans 8:28

It was a typical fall day in Grapevine in the fall of 2019. Fairly warm for October, leaves not even turning color yet. I was sitting in the front room of our house sewing, looking out a window overlooking the front yard. Coming from the field across the street, running—or limping, I should say—from north to south and through our yard and back into the woods was this dog. A rather large, German Shepherd-type looking dog, limping through. I ran outside to call him, but he just kept running. He was on a mission! I thought, "Oh, he must have gotten loose and is headed home. Poor boy has a hurt foot! I hope his owners get that looked at." He didn't look at me. He didn't even pause. He just ran.

That was that.

A couple of months later, in January 2020, I saw him again, running the same path as before. By the time I got outside, he was gone. I wondered where he might be going, not sure if I would see him again, but in March, I saw him once more. This time, he ran in the opposite direction from the woods, through our side yard, and to the north lot. Again, I ran out to see if he would at least stop to look at me. But no.

He was again intent on running and not stopping for anything. I felt terrible for him as his left front paw still looked injured. Maybe he had been hit by a car? Perhaps he just had something stuck in his foot? I thought I would never know.

I continued to see him now and then, as did other neighbors. Jonathan and Susan Hanold, my neighbors around the corner, even messaged me on *Nextdoor*, a website or app that is advertised as "a place to receive trusted information, give and get help, get things done, and build real-world connections with those nearby."

"Susan and I got home about two am last night, and there was a brown dog by your house. Kind of German Shepard looking. Pretty sure not a coyote. He appeared to have an injured back leg. Have you seen him around?"

"Yes! I see him about once a week now. He cuts through the back field and goes into the woods. I have run out to call him, and he runs off—acts a bit scared. He seems to be injured. He runs the same course from the north side of Foxfire down either side of our house and across the back into the woods, almost directly behind the cell tower. I have no idea whose he is, but I have been trying to get him to come!"

Now, I'm beginning to think he is no one's dog.

I continued to see him off and on all that year, but it was so random. I had to be looking out the window at just the right moment. If I was working in the gym, I might get lucky and see him out one of the windows that faces the woods. It was sporadic, maybe once a week at the very most.

While I wondered about him, I still didn't worry too much or give him a lot of thought as he didn't show himself much. This continued for the remainder of the year, although, to be honest, I didn't see him regularly enough to have him on my mind. For whatever reason, it just wasn't time.

After 2020, the year of the Covid-19 pandemic beginnings, I suppose we didn't think things would get much worse. In the great state of Texas, over 6 million cases of Covid-19 had been reported, with over 79,000 deaths. Worldwide? Over 362 million cases with over 5.6 million deaths. And counting. All because of this flu-like virus. For some, it was mild and inconvenient. But for the elderly or health compromised, it could be lethal. The pandemic was a tragedy in so many ways—people lost loved ones to the virus, businesses all over the country shut down, and people were unable to work. Small businesses suffered significant losses as they didn't have the resources to stay open. Our own training business was completely shut down for eight weeks, with only minimal people returning. It would take a couple of more months for people to feel it was safe. People were dying, yet families could not hold a funeral due to the regulations over the virus. People in hospitals for surgeries, yet family members were restricted from being by their side. Randy even had a client who had been married for over 60 years. Her husband was in the hospital with something unrelated to Covid-19, and she could not visit. Regulations wouldn't allow her in his room at all. After being in the hospital for over a month, he took a turn for the worse, and she watched him die from the other side of the window. She couldn't even be there to hold his hand. Others suffering from the loss of income and social interactions were suffering from depression. It was amazing what being home alone, not working, and not being able to gather with friends and family can do to people. Two of my children graduated from college during the height of the pandemic and lived at home with no job. Finishing classes online only, with no graduation ceremonies, and all aspects of college life stripped away, they didn't experience the usual thrill of the senior year in college. The excitement and anticipation of graduating and moving on in life had come to a halt. Why was this all happening?

Amid the turmoil, one thing among others began to stand out to people. Thankful hearts. Grateful hearts. Hearts of people realized the important things in life weren't their jobs or possessions but people. Spending time with loved ones or cutting back on the hours worked was beginning to resonate as "THIS is why this is happening!" Even on Facebook, people began posting positive things for a while—as if they suddenly realized there were more important things in life. I even saw this posted one afternoon:

Satan: "I will cause anxiety, fear, and panic. I will shut down businesses, schools, places of worship, and sporting events. I will cause economic turmoil."

Jesus: "I will bring together neighbors and restore the family unit. I will bring dinner back to the kitchen table. I will help people slow down their lives and appreciate what matters. I will teach My children to rely on Me and not their money and material resources."

BINGO.

It was as if God wanted to say, "Get your priorities straight." Not that I thought God caused this pandemic, and I certainly didn't blame Him. But I could see how He was using it in people's lives for good.

The shutting down of our country was difficult in so many ways. I never imagined that our church, Gateway, would close or that not meeting would be so heart-wrenching. It wasn't just Gateway; it was all churches. All businesses except those considered "essential" like grocery stores and pharmacies. At first, Randy and I were fine with "attending" church online. Over the months, we began to miss the gathering together. I had been a member of Gateway Church almost since its beginnings—over 21 years.

Randy was new to Gateway. When we married, he wasn't thrilled with the church. He liked small. He liked a little more traditional. Gateway had grown from a small group of people in our pastor's home to a multicampus church with over 100,000 in attendance every week. I began going to Gateway about the time of my divorce in 2000-2001. I had grown to love Gateway, the staff, the worship, the teaching—everything about it. I was faced with feeling as though I needed to find a church where Randy felt comfortable. A church that we could attend together and both enjoy and learn. I began visiting other churches, trying to find a place where I thought we would both thrive. But after about six months of attending other services, I hadn't found the answer.

Randy wasn't coming with me much of that time, so I finally decided to stay with Gateway. Why would I leave a church I loved when it seemed Randy wasn't that interested in finding a new place of worship? I continued to go to what I considered my church home.

During the next few months, Randy would attend with me for special occasions such as Easter or Mother's Day. And then something happened. He began to enjoy it! One Saturday afternoon, while I was taking a nap on the sofa, Randy came and woke me and said, "Stacie, do you want to go to the Saturday night service or wait till tomorrow?" I barely opened my eyes and moaned, "I'm waiting till tomorrow," wanting to finish my nap. I awoke 30 minutes later to find Randy gone. He had gone to church without me! At that moment, I realized he was beginning to like it. He was no longer going for me but himself. Over time, Randy came to love Gateway Church and our pastoral staff.

Robert Morris, the senior pastor of Gateway, has been such an incredible teacher and has allowed Randy and me to grow tremendously during our time there. During the pandemic, we were without. We could watch online. Worship online. Learn online. But it wasn't the same. It wouldn't be until August of 2020 that the church would re-open with strict rules for attending during the pandemic. That first Sunday back at church was life-changing. As we all began to sing together, we realized how much we had missed gathering with our fellow believers and friends. But for now, in early 2020, we were homebound. The pandemic was relentless and changed lives in ways during 2020 that we had never imagined.

If 2020 wasn't enough, maybe we needed a little more insight! Next? Welcome winter of 2021 in North Texas, a state where we get very little snow. Winter temperatures can get cold, but it can also be 80 degrees on Christmas Eve. When February of 2021 came and dumped so much snow, ice, and cold that our power grid went down, we were stunned. This would prove to be one of the state's worst natural disasters. Millions were left without power and were freezing in the darkness. Rolling blackouts for others, schools closed, and businesses shut down. Everything was blanketed with snow, ice, and single-digit temperatures. Wind chills below 0. This just doesn't happen in North Texas. Pipes were freezing all over town. Many homes had no heat or electricity for days! Stores were out of any bottled water as people flocked to the stores if they could even get out. With many homes having pipes freezing and breaking, the water had to be shut off to their homes, leaving them with none to drink or brush their teeth, let alone to try to cook something or flush a toilet. Later, when the snow would finally begin to thaw, flooding into homes due to those frozen pipes wreaked havoc for everyone, including insurance companies and contractors. Some families who had the means were checking into hotels in other areas, but even hotels were getting full. We just weren't prepared for this kind of weather. We never experienced below zero temperatures, waking up to extreme cold every day. Most winters, we don't even bother with a heavy coat. Hats and gloves? They are more for fashion than for practicality most of the time. People were bringing out every blanket, scarf, coat, and set of mittens, trying to keep themselves warm INSIDE their homes. For many, even this was not enough to stay warm.

Texas experienced 246 deaths from this winter storm, 2/3 of those due to hypothermia. People of all ages were affected as we lost souls ranging from 1 to 102. It was nightmarish. And this poor stray dog is outside all alone in this weather. Where could he be? How will he even survive? He most certainly will freeze to death.

I began urgently looking for him. Now that winter was here, and the trees were all barren of their leaves, it was much easier to see into the woods. Because of the heavy snow, no one was out. No one walking their dog. No one running. Not even raccoons scavenging for food. As I walked through the field behind my house, there they were. His little pawprints in the snow. I knew they were his because of his limp. They were easy to distinguish. Dressed in my winter gear, I followed the pawprints all over the property, analyzing his path. He had a route he ran every day, several times a day. Under barbed wire fences, through fields, into the woods, across the streets, his prints were everywhere. I bundled up for the five-degree weather and headed out to decide what the plan would be. First, water and food. I placed water and food bowls in five or six places, according to where I saw his tracks, not knowing if he would pass by them again. Within an hour, I would have to go back out to change the water. Frozen solid.

For days, I changed the water every 2-4 hours 'round the clock. I even started filling the bowls with hot water, knowing that it would very soon be cool enough to drink. The problem was whether he would find them in time.

Now is when a step counter would have been handy. I imagine I walked five miles a day those two weeks of cold and snow, just changing out his food and water. I would head out to check all the bowls, refill them, and head back inside. Within minutes it would be time to do it again. The cold was brutal. Relentless.

I didn't see another animal that entire time. Usually, we had deer, raccoons, coyotes, and even bobcats out behind our home. But not during this snow. They had to have been bedded down somewhere, trying to avoid the cold winds. I knew they were wild animals, but still, I worried for them. Every day during that storm, my sole purpose was to find this dog and see what I could do. Because my work was canceled due to the storm, I had the time. Even this downtime of no income was starting to look like it was working for the good.

Every morning, I had the horrible thought that I would find him somewhere, frozen. I couldn't imagine how this dog would stay warm enough to survive. With below zero wind temperatures, how could he? He didn't have a thick coat of fur. While he resembled a German Shepherd in coloring and size, he had more of the silky short coat that lays close to the body like a Great Dane or Dalmatian.

Plus, he was lean. Not just because of his breed but because he was out there on his own with no one feeding him regularly. Others were noticing him more now, with everything blanketed with snow. Pat Gray, the builder developing the land and building homes across from us, drove by with his grandchildren one day and spotted him in the field.

The grandkids yelled, "Look at that dog lying in the snow and ice!" Of course, they couldn't get him either—he ran. Still, more people had inquired about him on social media, having seen him running along the roads at some point. In fact, during the height of the snowstorm, someone posted on *Nextdoor*, asking about him:

Daron W, Southlake
Urgent Alert. Limping Dog in N Carroll Neighborhoods!! Brown and black short-haired German shepherd mix 214-***-****

Stacie Sauber, Southlake
I've seen this dog off and on for over a year and can't catch him! Do you have him or just saw him? I've tried everything to get him ... makes me so sad

13 Feb
Lynn M, Southlake
What area of Carroll? It's a pretty long street. Stacie, is it a stray? It is too cold for animals to be out.

13 Feb
Stacie Sauber, Southlake
I'm pretty sure he is a stray. I see him now and then, running from the field across the street (on Foxfire), then he goes through my side yard and back into the woods. I have tried to get him, but he is so scared. I saw him after Daron posted (across the street again), so I took food for him, but he saw me and ran. I also put a blanket in the garage of the house being built there as I see him occasionally rummaging around, probably looking for food. My heart hurts for him! He is really cute, but I'm not sure how to catch him.

13 Feb
Lynn M, Southlake
Stacie, I just sent you a PM (before I saw this), so you've answered some of my questions. Shoot. I hate to see these poor animals out and about by themselves.

13 Feb
Lynn M, Southlake
Shoot. OK. I'm going to start looking for him (her) and see if I can somehow catch it.

13 Feb
Daron W, Southlake
UPDATE We called 911 (due to animal control not being available) an officer came out saying they have tried catching this pup for over a year. He is very skittish and avoids everyone even though he is hurt. They even tried six officers at once but no luck. Police do not want to pursue it further because if the dog bites one of them, they would have to shoot him. So, they're allowing him to live his life. We spoke to someone in the neighborhood that has been placing food out for him. It is sad, but this pup has survived in this situation for a couple of years now.

13 Feb
Lynn M, Southlake
Well, I will try, but if so many ppl have already tried in the past, I probably will not have any luck either. Thanks for alerting everyone. Maybe more ppl will leave out some food and water, knowing he's out there and alone.

Lynn and I wrote off and on through the Nextdoor app during this harsh winter period. Lynne is an animal lover and truly wanted to help. She even brought us bags of food on occasion to contribute to helping this poor dog. On February 13, 2021, I messaged her to see if she had any advice.

Stacie
Hi Lynn, do you have any suggestions on how to catch him? I want to get him inside, even if it's just to Randy's shed out back. I have no idea whose he might be if anyone's. I don't know how to catch him other than lure him with food. But even when I take food out for him, he runs off. This has had me in tears. :-(Stacie

Lynn M, Southlake
Where do you normally see it? So, is it an actual stray, or does it belong to someone who just doesn't care? I can certainly try to catch it if I have an idea of where it is. So, do you know if it's a male or female?

Stacie
I have no idea if it belongs to anyone, but if it does, they don't deserve it! He has a hurt paw (don't know if it's a male), and he seems very sporadic. I see him at most once a week and never at a specific time. I just happen to see him running through my side yard and into the Corp property. He does go to the houses across from me as he appears to be looking for food that workers leave.

Lynn M, Southlake
OK, I'm going to start looking for it and see if I can somehow gain its trust and catch it. Breaks my heart. And limping? Is it normally limping when you see it? Also, where do you leave the food? Have you ever seen it eating it?

Stacie
It has been limping for a year! Front left paw, I think. I've never seen him eat, so for all I know, raccoons are getting the food. Let me know what I can do to help! I want this poor baby

to have a home. I have left food in the field east of my house and across the street by the home under construction, along with a blanket.

Lynn M
OK. Thank you for putting that blanket out. Hopefully, he or something will find it.

Stacie
Lynn, I'm home all day tomorrow and hoping this poor guy makes it through the cold. Call me if you need me—send me your number, and if I see him again, I'll call you! Maybe we can get him together.

Lynn M
Oh, I just realized I have your number already!
These next few days are just unthinkable temperature-wise for these animals. I'll run to Costco tomorrow and grab a bag of dog food. My number is 817.### ####... text or call anytime. I board my horses close to you (Lake Dr), so I'm in your area often. I only live about 10 minutes away off Peytonville anyway. I'll text you after Costco, and maybe you can show me the directions he heads. Thanks, Stacie.

Stacie
Sure thing! I've been out tonight at least a dozen times looking for him. I can't imagine being out in this.

Lynn
It's the worst cold I have felt in decades.

Lynn came by in the wintery, windy weather the next day with food, a giant box, and a blanket. We debated where to put it. We finally settled on a spot in the field behind my house, close to the path that he took. We crossed our fingers and prayed he would find it. It wasn't much, but maybe it would protect him from the fierce winds.

In the end, it didn't matter where we placed it. He wouldn't go into ANYTHING. The house across the street had since been torn down, and the two acres were being developed into three new homes. One of the homes where the builder, Pat and his wife Janet, were going to live was almost completed. The other home, right across the street from me, was up, windows in, doors in, but the garage was still open. I had put a blanket and food inside the garage, hoping he would at least find that and stay out of the snow. Watching with binoculars, he finally came by. He saw the food, ate it, and ran. I screeched, "Randy!! He found it! He found his food!" I was so elated he got the food, but he had no intention of going IN the garage. His instincts were to stay alert, have an escape, and stay alive. There was no way he would go into any shelter and feel trapped. He would rather be out in the open, cold, windy weather than take a chance of getting trapped, either by humans or by coyotes.

That same evening after dark, I grabbed the flashlight and went to the front yard. As I shined the high beam light across the street into the field, there he was. Two eyes glowing at me. He was curled up in the snow! My heart was breaking, but what could I do? If I took one step towards him, from ½ acre away, he would run. I decided to sit out on my front porch, swaddled in my blankets and coat, and watch him. He had to have someplace to sleep, but where? Ahh, the bamboo plants at the back of the lot. He had found a place with a tiny bit of bare grass to sleep where he could keep an eye out for predators and have a slight break from the howling north winds.

The next morning, I messaged my neighbor Jonathan again:

Stacie
Good morning, Jonathan; I have been trying to catch that stray dog that we have seen around here but to no avail. He is so scared! I saw him again last night in the field across the street from me as he tends to hang out over there. My guess is he is looking for leftover food from the workers. Anyway, he tends to run through the east yard at my house and back into the woods. I have set food out for him, but I have no idea if it's him getting it or just a raccoon! I could barely sleep last night, thinking of him out in this cold! The police even tried to get him at one point and couldn't, so they decided just to leave him be. Please keep your eyes out for him. Do you happen to have a kennel or cage or something that we could set up with blankets in the hopes that he might find it? I know it's a long shot, but my heart was breaking for this sweet boy.

Jonathan
Thank you for trying. My friend, a vet that lives nearby (the woman you probably see running by your home a lot), has tried a number of times to no avail. I know several rescue groups have also tried. Sorry, I don't have any kind of crate.

Stacie
Yes, I know Beverly—we saw him one morning while we were both out. I'm keeping my eye out for him but not sure what to do other than try to get him food and water.

Not sure of what else to do, I took another blanket over to his spot along with food and water. Randy also came through with a bale of straw. We took it over to where we saw him lying in the snow and made a nice straw and blanket bed for him. At least he could burrow down in it if he wanted. We did our best to create a warmer place for him. I would wake up in the middle of the night during that winter storm, wondering how he was doing. Crying. Lying there wide-eyed and unable to sleep. I could hear the wind in the trees and bushes. I could hear the sleet and snow hitting the windows.

I could only imagine where this poor dog was hiding out. During one of these nighttime awakenings, I came up with another idea. One that my husband, I know, thought was crazy, but it made sense to me. The next day, I took a t-shirt that I had been sleeping in over to his bed I had made and left it there. Maybe he will get used to my scent? Perhaps this will comfort him in some way? The following day, I went to check on him, and the t-shirt had been tossed aside! I put it back. Again and again, I took clothing over to his bed, hoping he would soon recognize me by my scent. I tried to think of anything I could do to reach this scared, lonely dog, but if several rescue groups had tried, what made me think that I could? I had never even had a dog, let alone known what to do with a dog. Little did I know this would begin a ten-month-long, daily, and often hourly activity from February through December.

Every morning and evening became a ritual of warming the blanket, bringing his food, and changing out the shirt, in hopes that he would have at least some sort of comfort. After a few days, the shirt was finally still on his bed. I found the blanket wadded up as if he had been sleeping on it. Success? I wasn't sure, but I was convinced he now could relate the smell of the shirt to me. About that time, he finally started eating his food each morning! I would take his food before the sun came up, knowing he was not yet gone. I tried to be quiet, sneaking up to get as close as possible, but he would always hear me, see me, smell me, then run. He would run fast and far. I'm not sure how long before he would come back to eat, but a few hours later, the food would be gone. Only his prints were in the snow, so I knew it was him and not some rascally raccoon getting the food.

(Although, as Randy often told me, "Stacie, the raccoons need to eat too!") Well, at least he now didn't have to look for food. One step at a time, I told myself.

Once he started eating what I brought him, he began not to run his routes as often. Randy thinks he must have been looking for food all that time. The discarded fast-food sacks from construction workers across the street weren't enough. Now he was getting regular meals. "WHY WON'T HE STOP RUNNING?" I thought. "He knows I'm bringing it. He knows I'm not hurting him. Still, he runs when he sees me coming. Doesn't he realize this is going to work for his good?" Even this early in my pursuit of this sweet dog, I would break down and cry. Daily. Multiple times a day, I would come in, only to cry to Randy, "Why won't he stop running from me?" Randy was always supportive, yet at this point, he was not as invested in my mission as I was. In time, he would be.

Chapter 3

"Fear not, for I have redeemed you;
I have called you by your name; you are Mine."

Isaiah 43:1

To see his routes, his paths, his very way of life, we put up a game camera. I thought if I could get an idea of when he came and from which direction, maybe it would help me with a plan. A few years earlier, I had purchased the game camera for Randy for Christmas. Behind our home, in the field and the woods, live several deer and other wildlife. I thought the camera would be a fun way of watching the deer, foxes, and bobcats, especially at night. It wasn't an expensive camera, but I had gotten recommendations from a client's husband, who has several cameras on his ranch property, about what to look for when buying one. Most game cameras are small, not much bigger than a large hand. They are very easy to operate and set up and easily hidden.

This one was camouflaged, so it blended into the trees quite nicely. If you didn't know it was there, you would probably never see it. For a while, we strapped it to a tree out back and were able to get several interesting and funny pictures of the deer eating, playing, chasing each other around. But after a couple of months, I suppose the novelty of the camera wore off, and we didn't use it much. But now we had a real use for it. Now I could put it to work for a cause and not simply for our enjoyment.

At first, the camera was across the street where I had put his blanket. Every night I would set it up, strap it to a nearby tree, and get pictures of him. Every morning at 5:00 am, it was a trip across the street to get the SD card. I was always so excited to see if he was there!

He seemed to be up more at night, roaming around the area. So was he mainly sleeping during the day? Was this normal? Or was it a way to avoid the coyotes and survive? Once awake in the early mornings, however, he would be gone. I had no idea where he was going, but he knew.

He had a survival plan. He may have been in survival mode, but I was in crying mode. The very thought of this poor dog being out in that weather made me sob. I had always loved animals, but since moving to this house with the property that surrounded us, I began to have even more of an affection for all animals—even the wildlife. I even started naming some of the wildlife. The regular deer that came to our yard and the wild turkeys that came gobbling at certain times of the year all had names. I told Randy if I named them, then no one could kill them. It's as if I felt that they belonged to us once they were given names. Randy, being the good sport that he is, joined with me in my fascination with the animals. We would sit in the sunroom at the back of our house and watch them all. They were beautiful to watch as well as humorous at certain times. The Tom turkeys strutting for the hens and the buck chasing the does during mating seasons were especially amusing.

With all the joy I had watching all the wildlife, I had never experienced this kind of grief over an animal. Seeing this dog outside in the snow and cold struck a chord. He wasn't a wild animal. He was a dog.

He had been someone's dog at some point and maybe even a much-loved pet. I didn't know his story, but I had to help him! I bundled up every day during that storm and walked the neighborhood looking for him. I would sit out on my porch, wrapped up in a cocoon of blankets, coats, and mittens. I would do anything to find him right now in this deadly cold. I had no idea why I was so obsessed with this dog, but I was. And Randy was along for the ride. He cared about the dog too, and was supportive of anything I wanted to do to help him. Even if it meant buying night vision binoculars!

Yes, my next step was buying the night vision binoculars in hopes of seeing him after dark. I had casually mentioned to Randy that I thought night vision binoculars would be a great way to see him after dark, thinking he would assume I was nuts. But instead, he said, "I think that's a great idea! Our sixth anniversary is coming up in a few weeks. How about we get each other the binoculars as an anniversary gift?" I couldn't believe my ears. He wanted to get them too! Maybe he was just doing this for me, or maybe he did want them. All I knew was Randy was the type of man who would do this just for me because he knew it would make me happy. I hopped online, did a bit of research, and decided on a pair that same day. I was so excited to get them! I guess in my mind I was purchasing goggles such as in the movie Patriot Games with Harrison Ford. I assumed I would be able to see him anywhere. After sitting outside, walking around with the binoculars and neighbors wondering what in the world I was doing, I realized they were not of any help. I could see with them, but not very far and not very clearly. They only made me look like I was trying to look into the homes of my neighbors.

At this point, I thought it wise to purposefully tell all my nearby neighbors what I was up to. Seeing someone with a flashlight and binoculars out in a field next to your home at midnight might be concerning to some. Fortunately, many had already figured out what was up. Many had seen this dog and had put two and two together when they saw me over on the vacant lot where he tended to hang out at times. The neighbors saw me so often in the field that it became almost expected. They would drive by, wave, and see me looking for the dog or taking water over to the field. Later, however, as I expanded my search for her, I would have to knock on a few doors and tell my tale. The conversations were usually about the same. "Hi, I wanted to let you know that I have been trying to find and help the stray dog you may have seen around the neighborhood the last few weeks," I would begin.

"Oh yes, we have seen him a few times. Do you know whose he is? And what is wrong with his paw?"

"No, all I know is he has been a stray for at least a year or more, and he wants nothing to do with people. I have been trying to provide food and water to him, but he is so skittish. He runs the minute he sees me. I don't know what he did to his paw, but if I ever catch him, I'd like to get him to the vet. Anyway, I wanted to let you know that if you see me out walking around with my binoculars, I'm not trying to peer into your home!"

Of course, we would all get a laugh out of that, and over the next several months, those neighbors would come to understand just how serious I was about trying to help this dog. As I said, I was obsessed. I wondered what this obsession might be doing to my family. What were they thinking? Did they think I was crazy? Did they support my efforts, or were they tired of hearing me talk about "the dog"? Randy, supportive as always, remarked that he was impressed with my passion for helping the dog. He saw the compassion and desire I had for helping this poor animal. Sydney, my adult daughter, who is temporarily living with us, mentioned that the only thing she was worried about was not me but the cats. She was concerned that if I ever did catch this dog and keep it, our cats wouldn't be able to adapt very well. They had been the only pets for nine years, and adding another animal to the mix at this point would be tough. Sydney has a heart for our cats and wanted to make sure adding a dog to the mix wouldn't cause too much anxiety for Rocky and Thomas. I fully intended to find this cute stray a home somewhere else because I, too, was concerned about blending these domestic cats with this wild dog that had been on his own for so long. Sydney never said much about it. She mentioned she was worried about the cats, but she also thought that maybe I needed something to take care of. My four children were grown and pretty much on their own, not requiring "mama's help" anymore. She figured maybe this was an outlet for me—a way to care for and take care of something else now that my children no longer needed me.

She never told me that until much later. All my family knew was that I felt like I had to get this dog some help!

The obsession began to run my life. My daily activities---my morning run or workouts, my work schedule, even my errands, all revolved around finding the dog. And by this point, "the dog" needed a name. I needed to know he was not just a dog, but he would be MY dog. What was I saying? I didn't even really want a dog! Because of this burden I had for him, I at least wanted to save him and find him a good home. I came in one morning after the snow was gone, and fortunately, Google did it again for me. "What are names for dogs that mean survivor or fighter?" Up popped a list of several names:

Anakin, meaning brave warrior. No, all I would think of would be Star Wars.

Ludwig, meaning strong and capable survivor. No, that sounds like an 1800's composer with a white wig.

Sarid, meaning survivor in Hebrew. No, it just didn't ring any bells for me.

And then I saw it: CLOVIS—One who fights for survival.

PERFECT!   I was so excited to find what I thought was the perfect name. I ran to tell Randy what I had come up with. When I told him and my daughter, Sydney, and my son, Mylon, they all had a similar reaction: "Clovis? What kind of name is that?" I think the kids even laughed a bit at the thought of naming a dog Clovis! Randy had suggested more common or popular names such as Jake or Lucky, but I felt like Clovis was the one. Lucky was just too cliché and common. I think I knew three other people with dogs named Jake. Clovis just fit—he was a survivor! Once again, Randy being the supportive husband he is, agreed that Clovis was the choice. From that day forward, we called him Clovis every chance we got. Of course, he didn't know what that was, but over time, he would learn. In time, he would come to know his name. I was sure that God already knew his name just as He knew mine.

It was about this time that I met another neighbor, Robby Ritchey. He and his wife, Paula, lived caddy cornered from me and across two roads. I hadn't had the chance to meet him but would see him out in his yard or on his driveway on occasion. One day, while I was walking and looking for Clovis, I saw Robby outside. I had seen Clovis run under his bushes that line the large culvert along the street, so I decided to introduce myself and see what he might know about him. We talked for at least 30 minutes, discussing what we both knew about this poor dog. He had seen Clovis off and on for a couple of years and had been putting food and water out on his driveway since the snowstorm. Good! Clovis has had ample opportunities for food. Robby mentioned time and time again that he considered Clovis to be a wild dog. "Stacie, I have seen wild dogs out in the country and in places in Oklahoma where I hunt sometimes. I think this dog is like a wild dog. I don't know if you could ever catch him or tame him. I have never in my life seen such a skittish dog! Paula and I can't even look at him without him running." This was exactly what I had experienced with Clovis up to this point, but something inside me said, "No, this isn't a wild dog. This is just a dog that needs to learn to trust." When I mentioned Clovis by name to Robby, he said, "Oh, you mean Hank? I've been calling him Hank."

By the end of February, the brunt of our winter was over. It was still cool and often fairly cold, but nothing like early February. I still worried about Clovis out in the weather and the darkness, all alone and scared. But at least the freezing temperatures were gone. Of course, it seemed there was always something. Rain. Wind. Hail. In Texas, we get a lot of hail during certain seasons. We have been known to have hail ranging in size from a pea to a softball! This type of hail, if you have never experienced it, can wreak havoc on just about everything. It ruins thousands of cars every year by pummeling the body as well as breaking windshields. It damages roofs of homes and destroys landscaping. It can kill if one is caught out in it with no protection. Yes, I worried for Clovis in every condition. Randy would always try to tell me that he had probably found shelter somewhere. "Stacie, he is smart. He knows where to go. I'm sure he has a hiding spot or a shed that he goes to."

Yes, Randy always tried to make me feel better, but I'm not sure he believed what he was saying.

Throughout the next several months, Robby continued to put food out. His house is on a one-acre plot, with most of the yard being north of his home. I later discovered that this is where Clovis was going much of the time. He would sleep in the far corner of his yard. Robby had no fencing on the south side of his home, and there was a big gap in the fencing on the north side. Clovis had his escape routes. He knew how to get out of there if needed. I wish I had known this earlier, but it wouldn't be until the heat of summer that I would find his hiding spot.

Over the months, Robby and I had a few conversations about Clovis. Because he was convinced Clovis was a type of wild dog that wasn't hurting anyone or damaging anything, he had decided to pretty much leave Clovis alone. He still put food and water out, but any attempt at luring him or catching him was moot in his mind. Robby said so many people had tried to catch Clovis but to no avail. One afternoon, a gentleman and his daughter saw Clovis running through the yards. They stopped to speak to Robby about his wandering dog. When Robby told them, "Oh, he isn't my dog. He just hangs out around here and lies in my yard sometimes. He's not hurting anything, and besides, no one can catch him," the man acted stunned. How could you NOT be able to catch a dog lying in your yard?

Before Robby knew it, the police were there. The man called them to come out and see about this poor dog. When the officers arrived, they almost grinned as if they had seen this dog before. Several times. This wasn't the first time someone had called about Clovis, and it wasn't the first time the police had shown up. They, too, informed the man and his daughter that the dog was not catchable.

Earlier that year, two officers came out to try to catch Clovis, but they were unsuccessful. When other officers heard that the first crew couldn't catch him, they almost sarcastically said, "Let's go show them how it's done." But no, they couldn't get him either. Finally, a third police unit arrived with yet two more officers. So now, three cars and six officers, all trying to catch this stray dog with a limp. In some ways, it had to be humiliating that this dog eluded them. Radios in hand, messaging each other as they tried to surround him, Clovis still managed to escape. The officers finally said to let him be. He wasn't rummaging through trash. He hadn't been aggressive to anyone, nor had he shown a single sign of any behavior that would warrant them capturing him. They did note that if they continued to try to catch him, and he did bite one of the officers, they would have to put him down.

So, Clovis was left to roam.

Robby and the officers believed that Clovis would be OK. At least as OK as a stray dog can be.

Besides, Clovis was smart! He was so incredibly smart. He had not just survived on his own, but he had avoided getting hit on busy roads. Avoided being caught by countless people. Avoided coyotes. Now he was avoiding me. I still couldn't figure out why was he avoiding the person who was bringing him food and water. The person who was speaking softly and calmly to him. The person who was thinking about him day and night. While I was pondering this, the thought ran through my mind--which I knew was from the Lord—"You know how you are providing for Clovis? That's how I always provide for you. Just like you have named him and call to him, I call to you in the same way. You wonder why he runs from you, but why do you run from ME?" I was stunned, but even with that revelation, my mind came right back to the problem in front of me. Clovis wouldn't come to me, and I wondered if Robby might be right. Maybe he was just a wild dog that would never be tamed. Maybe he would never come to me. Sometimes I did feel like I was trying to catch a coyote. An animal that needed food but didn't want anything to do with human contact. He had suffered some kind of trauma. What could have possibly happened to him? Had he been abused? Had he been dumped? Had he simply gotten lost and gone into some sort of survival mode? Maybe I didn't want to know. Trying to catch Clovis was about as easy as trying to catch a wild animal. This was no ordinary stray that could be coaxed into your arms with a bowl of food or a tasty treat. This was a dog who trusted no one and maybe never would.

Robby and Paula weren't the only ones helping to care for Clovis. Next door to Robby, just to the north, lived Tim and Julie Lamont and their two girls, Georgia and Olivia. They lived in a house belonging to a church on the property. I would estimate there were about 5 acres surrounding their house, mostly fields and some huge oak trees. Clovis must have loved that he had so much space and so many outlets for escape.

By mid-March, trees are budding, and everything is starting to blossom. Spring begins early here, and I was happy that Clovis might have better places to sleep and hide. We began to see him lying out in front of their home.

One morning on my walk, looking for him, I saw him lying in a drainage ditch in a pile of leaves in front of their house. Of course, the minute he saw me, he ran. STOP RUNNING! As summer approached, Tim and Julie began putting big buckets of water out for him. He would sprawl out in their yard, and it would seem that this would be an easy catch. Tim and Julie even mentioned that cars would stop and come to their door to tell them their dog was loose. When the caring bystanders were told Clovis was a stray and unable to be caught, they would never believe it. "We will try to get him!" Tim and Julie would smile as if to say, "Go right ahead. Give it your best shot," knowing that it was an impossible feat.

Definitely not an easy catch at all.

Did I mention he was smart? That little Clovis could be lying there sleeping one minute and the next minute be gone. How he could get away so quickly I will never understand. Besides, what would we do if we caught him? Tim and Julie had no fenced yard to keep Clovis in, and he would most likely panic and maybe bite anyone who tried to grab him. He never seemed aggressive, but we had no idea what that poor dog had been through and how he would respond. I told everyone I spoke to early on, "I'm trying to be patient and let HIM catch ME. I don't want to scare him or let him think I'm after him. In time, he will come to me if I'm patient enough." Tim and Julie understood that completely. They, too, wanted to see him caught and in a good home, but watching him from their yard, they knew all too well why I was approaching Clovis in this manner.

It was the same thing day after day. Get up at five, check the camera, go for my run or walk and look for the dog. Call for the dog—"CLOVIS!" I would see him in so many places. At times, he hung out on the east side of our house, and neighbors would see him peeking out of the woods near the street. This area was shady, protected, and safe from people. Clovis would lie back in the trees, trying to get a good nap.

Randy and I noticed the he would come from the north side of our street, run behind the new houses being built opposite of our home, and then dart across the road and crawl under a barbed-wire fence.

On a few occasions when we saw him a little closer through a window or with the game camera, he appeared to have some sort of injury on his back, just between the shoulder blades. It looked like he had gone under that barbed wire fence too many times, scraping himself as he went. Randy was the hero this time and went over to clip the fence a bit so he could get under it easier. At least now, he wouldn't scrape himself. I was worried about his injury, hoping it wasn't infected, but what could I do?

I caught so many other good photos and videos of Clovis on my game camera. I also found out I was feeding an entire army of raccoons! I bet we have the fattest, most well-fed raccoons in town now. They were proving to be a huge menace to my plan. Every night, four to five of these critters would make their way to our front yard or wherever I had put the food bowl that night. Because we have motion sensor lights on our carport, which is just outside our bedroom window, I would see the lights pop on just after dark, announcing to me that someone or something was out there. I would peek out the blinds to see an entire family of them, seemingly tiptoeing across the driveway, making their way towards the food! I'd jump out of bed, running to the door to try to scare them away.

I probably scared Randy more than the raccoons, waking him as I jolted out of bed, rushing out the front door, and clappping my hands while hollering at the raccoons. This was only a temporary fix, though, and they would soon return for their meal. Sometimes Clovis would beat them to the food. Most nights, however, those rascals had a feast. I began sitting out on the front porch glider, and as the raccoons would come creeping through the yard looking like bandits, I would shine a high-powered flashlight at them. They would run like crazy, but within minutes, they would be back, trying their scheme again. This would go on for upwards of an hour. I would often give up and go inside as it was getting late. I was probably scaring Clovis away, who was probably watching this showdown from across the street. After about a month of trying to chase the raccoons away every night, I searched for a different method—Peppermint spray. Yes, I read that peppermint spray was good for keeping rodents away as well as raccoons or squirrels. So, thanks to Amazon, I ordered a gallon of the liquid and put it in a spray bottle.

Now, I would win this battle! Sitting on the porch, waiting for the unsuspecting food thieves, almost made me giggle. And then they would approach. At first, I sprayed an area of the ground around the blanket and food bowl, hoping it would deter their efforts. It didn't.

So, what was next but to spray them directly? I didn't want to hurt the raccoons! I just wanted them to leave Clovis' food alone. One brave and determined varmint would walk right up to me. Sitting about three feet away, I would spray the peppermint right in that raccoon's face, but he just looked at me as if to say, "Is that all you got, lady?" I must admit those little guys were so cute. My frustration would quickly turn to chuckles, as the brave little raccoons stared me down. I know they were laughing at me. Just as my neighbors probably were as well. Oh, yes. Randy, too.

I'm sure he thought I was now losing my mind. Every time I would jump out of bed to intersect them, I could almost hear him groan and then laugh at me for even trying. Randy knew they were driving me crazy. These raccoons were my biggest problem for a long time. My last effort was to give them their own food. I began setting two additional bowls of dog food out—one on the east side of the house and one on the west. These would be right in their paths as they made their way to the front yard where Clovis' bowl was located. Maybe this would deter them and give him a chance to get to his food. It worked on occasion, but in the end, I think I just made an entire family of raccoons very happy. And to be honest, not only were they extremely adorable, but it made me happy to know they were getting fed as well. Opossums, skunks, foxes, and bobcats all showed up on the camera, but not like those raccoons. On many occasions, I even commented to Randy, "I feel like I could get those raccoons to come to me easier than Clovis!"

I'm sure I was right.

I decided to move the camera to different locations every few days to get an idea of where Clovis was and where he was going. The camera was fairly easy to move but finding the right spot was the trick. I needed a tree or post to strap the camera to and then angle the camera in just the right direction where I thought Clovis would be coming from. Thank goodness Costco sells huge packs of AA batteries as we were going through those like wildfire. It was worth it. The camera was my eyesight and was doing a great job. Clovis was everywhere. So was a mischievous coyote. I still haven't determined if they were friends or foes, but Clovis and the coyote would be on camera together. It was as if they were playing a game of tag at the food bowl. At least I knew that Clovis was either getting away, defending himself, or making friends!

Still unsure if Clovis was a girl or a boy, I finally hit the jackpot on the camera one night. That little Clovis came right in front of the camera and squatted. It was as if he wanted the camera to get a good view. GIRL. TOTALLY GIRL.

It was too late. We had been calling her Clovis for so long (which honestly sounded more like a boy's name) that we decided we just had to keep it. It had become her name. She was really one who fought to survive.

Chapter 4

"But you, be strong and do not let your hands be weak, for your work shall be rewarded!"

2 Chronicles 15:7

Not only did my game camera get some incredible shots at night of all Clovis' activities, but it also proved to be quite helpful in discovering our food bowl thief. I had been putting food out for Clovis across the street where she slept, but once the really cold winter was over, I started putting her food dish in our front yard, trying to lure her to my house. I tried putting it in several places, always trying to find what I thought would be the ideal spot.

I knew she wanted some privacy, but she also needed escape routes. I knew she wanted to be away from the roads, but she didn't want to be too close to the house or the woods behind us. I had to try to think like a wild dog.

Directly behind our home are fields that are open with a few trees. About 50 yards back, however, are the woods. These woods are part of the Corp of Engineers and City of Southlake property that runs from behind our home down to Grapevine Lake, about a mile away. A small creek runs through the woods, and while it only has a trickle of water, at times, it can be quite full, supplying all the wildlife with necessary water. The woods themselves are not forest-like as you would see in a mountainous, lush area. These woods, while thick, are rather scroungy. The trees are tall but slim, and many have briars and thorns two to three inches long, with some up to five inches in length.

The many mesquite trees that grow there are the real villainous thorn producers. A fallen branch with the long, piercing thorns would make a great weapon as they are strong and hard. They don't break off easily and could cause severe damage if you're not careful. I have stepped on these, piercing clear through my sneakers to my foot. Not good for little animals not wearing shoes! There are a lot of underbrush and vines, which like to grab at your legs as you walk through. There are some paths back in these woods, simply from the deer and coyotes who follow their same patterns every day. Randy and I have, on occasion, walked back into the woods, looking for deer antler shed or even just picking up trash that has blown through the fields and into the trees. It's a gem of a place for animals to live, as it's nestled into the town.

While so much land is being taken away to build homes and businesses, this small strip is a haven for many wild animals. Clovis would run through those woods, headed where we had no idea. Maybe it was to find water at the creek. Maybe it was to cut through to homes on the neighboring roads where she was finding more scraps of food. Either way, it couldn't be too safe at night with all the coyotes. I think Clovis realized this! So, when contemplating where to place her food bowl each day, I took these things into consideration.

"If I were Clovis, where would I want it?" I would think to myself. Randy and I would walk around the house, discussing options. "Where would you want it if you were a dog, Randy?" We would have the same discussion over and over, never really knowing where to put it. Once we decided on a location, I laid out a blanket with her food bowl, a treat, and some water. I would wake up to find the entire bowl missing. I was using a lightweight plastic storage container for now since I had no real dog food bowl. But where was it? Had it blown away? I looked all over the yard, but it was gone. Across the street, I went to the field where I would see her lying at times, and there it was. Behind a large rock pile at the latest construction site was Clovis' dish. To confirm my suspicions, I went inside to check the game camera card. Jackpot!

Clovis had carried off her food bowl across the street to eat behind the rock pile in secret. Maybe she felt safer there than in our front yard, exposed as cars drove by. Maybe she was sneaking off with it before the raccoons could get it? I was just glad she got her dinner.

Clovis had a way about her. She was fun to watch on camera. I wish I knew what was going through her mind! After dark, and usually between 10 pm–2 am, she would make her way to my yard, eat her food if the raccoons had not beaten her to it, all while constantly scanning side to side for predators, and then when finished, she would look around, snatch up her treat, and RUN. It was as if she had been saving it for dessert and she wanted to take it to go.

She acted like it was a game. Maybe she was going back to her bed, or perhaps she was collecting and burying the treats somewhere. She did seem to be excited to get them! I was giving her a small "triple kabob" treat made of bits of meat. She thought it was a delicacy. I moved the camera every few nights along with her blanket and food bowl, testing to see if she would find them and what she would do.

She always managed to find the food, and once in a while, she would lay down on the blanket for a few minutes. But then, she was gone. I guess she felt she had to keep moving. After all, a sitting, stationary target is much easier for a coyote or other critter to approach or attack. As I have said, she was such a smart little girl.

One night, I captured video of her eating her dinner. While eating, a skunk approached, tail raised straight up. Clovis looked up, and when the skunk reached about 6 feet away from her, she took off! I imagine she had learned the hard way at some point, but she knew. She knew that she was no match for the scent of a skunk!

By this point in our adventure, I was spending a lot of time outside watching for her—binoculars in hand at all times. The binoculars I had also purchased for Randy for Christmas one year to watch the wildlife in our backyard were now proving their worth with Clovis.

Thankfully, because I work from my home and have gaps in my schedule, I had the ability to look for her. I had the time that many others who also cared about her probably didn't have. I took every chance I had to take a walk or to sit on my porch, even if just for 10 minutes. Many mornings after my run or walk, and most afternoons, I would hop on my bike and ride the neighborhood, looking for her as I rode. It was much quicker this way, and I could cover more ground than by foot.

Just as I did while on my walks, I would pray while on my bike. Not just for Clovis, but my family, for my children. The more I prayed for Clovis, the more it seemed that God would speak to me about my children, reassuring me that just as I was taking care of Clovis and looking out for her, He was doing the same thing for my family.

It was always a much-needed confirmation to me that He was and is in control. So, there I would be, riding my bike, praying, singing, and looking. And yes, even then, always with my binoculars. The binoculars enabled me to see her a little more closely. I couldn't see details about her injured paw, but it didn't seem to be getting worse. It also didn't appear to cause her pain. At least, she didn't make any expressions or vocalizations about it. She walked with her front left paw lifted, rarely touching the ground. I was tired of seeing this poor girl injured and alone.

I was also beginning to get plain tired. Tired physically and emotionally. I am a creature of habit and routine, almost always going to bed at night and getting up the next morning at the same time every day. Partly due to my job and my workout routine, and partly because I love a regular schedule. Staying up later than usual to watch for Clovis in the dark was starting to take a toll on my sleep. Still getting up at 5:00 am, I was getting a bit worn. Not only that, but for all the work I was putting in, I felt I was reaping no reward. Clovis now had food, but my plan was going so incredibly slow. It messed with my emotions, my mind. I was tired of walking all over the neighborhood every chance I got. I was tired of feeling useless and ineffective. I was tired of the tears. Crying can be so physically exhausting! At times I wanted to give up. Maybe I never would catch her. Just how long is this going to take? But then I would remember God's patience with ME. His waiting on ME. His pursuit of ME. Galatians 6:9 would come to mind: "And let us not be weary in well-doing, for, in due season, we shall reap, if we faint not." So, I had to continue. I also kept reminding myself that God would never give up on me. So how could I give up on this sweet, lonely dog?

I began to sit on our front porch every chance I got now, not just during my work breaks. I would eat breakfast there, read my Bible there, do any paperwork I could out there—to be able to keep my eyes open for her. Scrolling through my phone was my next pastime as I waited on her. Lunch? Out on the porch. Dinner? Same thing.

Any opportunity I got, I was out there waiting to catch a glimpse of her. I continued sitting outside after dark, hoping she would come to get her food while I was there. I'm sure my neighbors thought that all I did was sit on my front porch, staring out my binoculars. "There is that woman again, just sitting there watching cars go by!" I could hear it in my head. I would put her food and treat out in the yard on top of a blanket, then sit on the glider on my porch just waiting. Sometimes for over an hour at a time. Poor Randy. He would be inside, ready for bed, but I would be outside waiting for Clovis. He understood. I know he understood. But I also think that he thought maybe I was wasting my time. Was I?

Even though Randy wasn't fully participating in this quest yet, he was allowing me to pursue Clovis however I felt I should.

While he didn't help at this point in the daily feedings and searching, he was proud of what I was doing. I could tell. I would hear him telling his family over the phone about it. I would hear him telling a client about how his wife was so dedicated to rescuing this dog and how he could see the compassion I had for her. Yes, he was proud. And soon, he would be right there alongside me. But for now, I was alone. Waiting on Clovis outside in the dark, alone.

Often, while waiting out in the dark by myself, I would begin to pray, talking to God about Clovis and what was going on. I knew that God was aware of everything, but I felt the need to fill Him in on everything I was doing as though He had missed something. I knew that while I sat on the porch alone, I wasn't truly alone. God is omnipresent. He is with us all the time. Every day. Every minute and every second.

Sometimes, however, we aren't aware of His presence. Even in the darkness of night, waiting on Clovis, I knew that He was with me, guiding me on what to do next. I couldn't figure out or understand why this was consuming me the way it was or why God had put this dog in my path, to begin with. Why was it taking so long? What could the reason possibly be?

On a couple of occasions during those late-night porch sessions, Clovis would sneak up to eat her food while I was there. Could Clovis be starting to let her guard down and not be quite so scared? She had to know I was there. She had to be able to smell me from 15 yards away. I would sit there so silently, almost holding my breath so as not to move, not wanting to scare her. I wanted her to see that I had no intention of coming toward her. She would eat, grab her treat, and run back across the street. She was playing a game with me, it seemed. It was also as if God was saying, "I hear you loud and clear, Stacie. I'm still here, and I am still orchestrating this entire rescue. Here's a little victory for you tonight." And I needed that so desperately. I needed to know that everything I was doing wasn't just a waste of my time. I would eventually have to go inside and go to bed because I had to get up early. I would sit outside as long as I could before finally giving in to my tiring eyes. Before I knew it, my alarm would go off again at 5:00 am and I would start all over again. Every. Single. Day.

It was about this time that our neighbor, John Olson, and I began talking about Clovis. He had seen her, of course, as many in our neighborhood had. I filled him in on my escapades and how badly I wanted to help her. He and his wife, Ginger, are dog lovers, and he told me, "Stacie, if you ever catch her, I would love to adopt her if you aren't going to keep her."

"That would be awesome, John! I mean, we have two cats, and I don't know how they would handle it all. I've never really wanted a dog, but I feel the need to help this one. If I ever get her, that would be so fantastic! She would have a good home and still be in my neighborhood so I could come to see her."

One of the main drawbacks to keeping her myself was, of course, our two cats. Rocky and Thomas, as I mentioned, are both around nine years old and very set in their ways.

Rocky, the large, dominant Maine Coon cat, will let you know that this is his territory. He will sit out in the backyard at the gates to our fence, watching people walk by with their dogs. He is on high alert when one comes close. Let's say that dogs are not among his favorite things. My daughter, Natalie, has a 12-year-old sweet Bassett named Bodie. Rocky has been around Bodie for his entire nine years off and on. Natalie will bring Bodie over to our backyard, and you would think that Rocky was demonic! Not only does he ruffle up and hiss as many cats would, but he growls—I mean a loud guttural growl, sounding like he is about to attack. At times, he would try to break through the sliding doors in our sunroom to reach Bodie. He was not going to have this dog in his yard! He was even known to push open the French doors of one room to attack Bodie. We had never seen anything like it. Rocky, all 22 pounds of him, would go from window to window, watching and growling at Bodie. And honestly, growling isn't even an adequate word for what was coming out of this cat!

It was a screeching, howling type of noise that I had never heard from a cat. There was no doubt in our minds that if we let them be in the same room together, Rocky would attack Bodie with a vengeance. He was genuinely distressed. He was upset the entire time Bodie was at the house.

Rocky couldn't get used to a dog being at our home. He didn't like Natalie being in our home at times either. Rocky probably associated Natalie with Bodie and, on a couple of occasions, tried to attack Natalie! Thomas was a bit more indifferent. He would go into another room or hide under the bed. Not Rocky. He was making it known that this was HIS house, HIS yard, and HIS family.

No dog was going to come and mess with him. With this in mind, we thought that finding Clovis a home, such as with John and Ginger, would be the perfect answer. We didn't want to cause trauma to the pets we already had, and we certainly didn't want Rocky attacking Clovis. Sydney was relieved when I told her we probably wouldn't keep Clovis as she was extremely sensitive to the cats. We did not want to disrupt or upset them.

I thought I would have to give Clovis away. For the moment, I was OK with that. I thought.

Little did I know that she would eventually have such a grasp on my heart that there would be no way on earth I would give her up. Not even to this wonderful family that had offered.

I thought I had spent a lot of time up to this point searching for Clovis. The next few months proved to be even more time-consuming and emotionally draining. It was consuming my life as I looked for her every day, but I couldn't give up.

Chapter 5

"Be anxious for nothing, but in everything by prayer
and supplication, with thanksgiving,
let your requests be made known to God."

Philippians 4:6

W atching Clovis during the day with the binoculars and at night by camera, we could tell how nervous and anxious she was at times. Her constant head turning side to side while she was eating—she was on high alert. Always.

Fight or flight had been turned on for Clovis, and I wondered if she got any real rest. Peaceful rest. Rest without having to look over her shoulder and wonder if someone or something was coming. It was my biggest concern for her. The mere fact that she was constantly on the run and frightened made me sadder than anything. Now that the weather was warmer and she was getting food, my concern had moved to her mental status. I just wanted this sweet girl to have peace. And so, I began praying for Clovis. Not that I hadn't been doing that all along, but I earnestly started praying that God would give her rest.

I believe God honors prayers for our pets just as He does our prayers for anything in our lives. Philippians 4:6 says, "Be anxious for nothing, but in everything by prayer and supplication, with thanksgiving, let your requests be made known to God." Everything. Even Clovis.

After all, who created animals?

Who created my little Clovis? If I cared so deeply for this stray dog, surely God cared as well. I started to feel like the Lord was using this dog to show me just how much He cares for His creation—Clovis as well as me. So of course, I would pray for Clovis.

Not only was I praying for her, but soon we would have numerous neighbors and church members praying too. To some, this might seem a bit silly or trivial.

But it wasn't to me. And I'm quite sure it wasn't to God. He created Clovis. He was looking out for Clovis. He had placed me in her life, or her in mine, for a reason. I didn't know how or when this would all come together, but God had a plan. He was watching out for Clovis and even had strangers offering food for her. Again, *Nextdoor* was the avenue that came through. Someone had posted that they had just lost their sweet dog, and they had food leftover that they were willing to give away:

> 4/20
> Stacie
> Hi Noah, I'm so sorry to hear of the loss of your dog. They are family! I have been trying to catch a stray (wild!) dog for a long time now, and I feed her daily, but she won't come near—eats in the middle of the night! Anyway, if no one else has spoken for your dog food, I'd love to have it for my poor stray. Stacie
>
> Noah
> Hi Stacie, sorry I'm just now getting back. The food is still available for you to take if you're still interested. Will be out and about tomorrow, so can drop it off, or you can pick up in Grapevine. Let me know. Thanks.
>
> Stacie
> Oh, that's fantastic, Noah. Thank you! Either way is fine—-I can swing by tomorrow between 2-5 if that works or if you want to drop it off. I'm on Foxfire Lane—-just off Dove and Lonesome Dove. Don't go out of your way, though. I can come by if you aren't over this way.
>
> Noah
> No problem! Going to plan to drop it off around noon tomorrow if that works for you?
>
> Stacie
> That's perfect, thank you! I work from home in the building at the back and will be here, so just call when you get here, or you can leave it under the carport. My sweet stray dog thanks you!!

We had others donate food as well! Our neighbors, Brian and Donna Earle, had also recently lost one of their dogs, Blackjack. They so graciously offered their leftover food to us for Clovis. I know it couldn't have been easy for them during that time, but their willingness to help another dog was very heartfelt. In the same way, our clients, Fred and Amy Hondzinski, lost their dog, Gordie, about the time of the great snowstorm in February. They provided us with food and treats for Clovis, all while grieving the loss of their pet. A few months later, yet another woman from *Nextdoor* donated food to us! I saw people who knew us and those who didn't come together for the sake of this dog. Randy said the whole neighborhood was beginning to pull together. It was heartwarming to know so many people genuinely cared for Clovis.

As we continued to pray for her and try to earn her trust, I decided to bring this to my Bible study friends. I was apprehensive as I had only known these women for three to four weeks. What would they think? Aren't there "real" problems to pray about? My mind was telling me not to mention it, but my heart said I had to.

I had joined this ladies' Bible study at my church, Gateway. We were meeting on Wednesday night at The Corner Bakery, a small café in the Southlake Town Center. After our discussion came prayer requests. We went around the table, expressing our needs and asking for prayer. I heard the other ladies' requests.

Requests for prayers for marriages, finances, and healing of loved ones. How could I even ask for prayer for a dog?? It was my turn.

"I know you all might think this is crazy, but there is this dog…." And I began to tell them the story of Clovis. "I don't know why I'm so obsessed with getting this dog, but I am. It's consuming me, and I so want to help her. It's all I think about!" Tears welling up in my eyes.

One woman in our group, Patty Huckabee, looked directly at me and said, "Stacie, God put Clovis in your life for a reason. You are like the Holy Spirit to Clovis. Just like you are going after Clovis to save her—that's how God is going after your daughter."

It hit me deeply. Profoundly. So much so that I couldn't get it out of my head. My children were all raised in church and loved the Lord. Three of them, Sydney, Felice, and Mylon, still serve Him fervently. But my oldest, Natalie, turned away from our beliefs when she went to college. Natalie is a wonderful young woman now. Don't get me wrong. At 31 years of age, she is independent, friendly, hardworking, caring, and compassionate towards people. I couldn't be prouder of her heart for people. However, she lost her belief in God, or rather in Jesus. As a Christian mother, this hurts my heart more than anything. I will continue to believe that she will come back to the Lord until the day I die, but that doesn't mean it's easy. I worry for her.

I pray for her. I love her deeply and always will. There is absolutely nothing that will ever change my love for her. And now, hearing Patty tell me that God had put this stray dog in my life as an allegory to Natalie made me cry. It hit me hard. Once again, the Lord said to me, "This is how I feel about the lost and those who have fallen astray. I have never-ending patience and will never give up on them. I will never try to trap anyone as I want them to come to Me when they are ready."

God was going after Natalie the way I was going after Clovis. Patiently and with kindness. Compassionately and with love. Not forcing her, not trying to trap her. Wanting her to come to Him just like I wanted Clovis to come to me. I didn't want to trap Clovis, and God wasn't going to "trap" Natalie. He wants her to come to Him because she sees His goodness, His kindness, His provision, and His protection.

I will never forget that night of Bible Study.

Those words rang through my head almost every day from that night on. From that day forward, every time I felt discouraged about finding Clovis or getting her to come to me, I thought of those words that Patty spoke. How could I give up or turn aside from this dog who desperately needed a home? How could I not find time to look for her? How could I just quit because I was exhausted? I had to pursue her. I had to bring her home.

Shortly after the experience with my Bible Study ladies, Randy and I ran into Jerry David. Jerry works for Pat, the builder who now lives across the street from us and who was building the new houses in our neighborhood. Randy had talked with Pat on several occasions and had met Jerry, his right-hand man. Both of them were believers. Their crew would meet for prayer at Pat's house every day at 3:00 pm. Soon, they would be praying for Clovis too. We spoke to Pat and Jerry about Clovis, as she spent so much time on the properties they were working on. We wanted them to know we were trying to woo her. Trying to earn her trust. The last thing we wanted was for anyone, even out of a good heart, to try to catch her or trap her. I didn't want to do anything that would make her digress or trust us less. They agreed and told their construction crews what was going on. Good.

At least now all those men realize I'm not just a crazy woman wandering around the construction zone with binoculars.

As we talked with Jerry that day, telling him about my passion for this dog, he said to me, "Well, you are acting like the Holy Spirit. That's exactly how the Lord is with us." I told him what Patty had said to me during that Bible study meeting. It was confirmation. He said that the way I was pursuing Clovis was how God pursues us. Relentlessly. It's how He pursues everyone. He doesn't want us to come to Him out of obligation, guilt, or fear, but out of love.

Randy and I casually asked Jerry to keep Clovis in his prayers, and he said, "Well, let's pray right now! Father, we pray for this dog, Clovis, and ask that you watch over her. Help her not to be scared. Just as you turned the heart of a king, you can turn the heart of this dog. In Jesus' name, Amen." AMEN! Wouldn't you know, one to two minutes later, there she was. Coming through the lot across the street in the middle of the day was Clovis. It was as if God wanted me to know He had heard. And I know that Pat, Jerry, and their crew continued to pray for Clovis.

It was from that point on that everything in my life turned toward this sweet dog. I say sweet because Clovis never appeared to be aggressive. She never growled or barked. I never heard a single vocalization out of her.

It was as if she was remaining quiet so as to not draw attention to herself. Maybe that was part of her survival skills? If she didn't draw attention to herself, maybe she would be left alone. For whatever reason, Clovis was quiet and rather calm for a dog. I'm sure she was afraid and tired of running and hiding, but she seemed unusually calm. I never even considered that she might bite me or attack me. Because of this, I had no fear of trying to approach her.

I was careful and cautious, but not out of fear. Out of respect. I wanted Clovis to see that I would be good to her. That I would treat her well. That I would provide food and water. And that she would have warmth in the winter through straw and blankets. I also wanted her to see that I would leave her alone.

I wanted her thoughts to be, "This woman is bringing me food! She's even talking to me and being kind. But then she leaves! She's not trying to trap me!" Yes, that's what I wanted to see play out in her mind.

So, as I began my quest for her with even more vigor, if that was even possible, I made the decision never to be a predator to her. I wasn't out on a conquest. Rather I was out as a suitor and how he would treat his love. Kindly and with sweet deeds. This would make her want to come to me, I believed. Would it work?

My routine was already in place, but now it became more frequent. Every morning at 5:00 am, check the game camera. Did she come and eat? If not, which critter got her food this time? Oh, look! She came back by three or four times last night! She knows there is food waiting for her, at least. After camera check, I went out for my morning run and then hopped on the bike. At this point, my eyes are scouring every place I go, trying to see if I can find where she spends her time. On mornings that I would run, I would keep my eyes open for her, but it was usually too early and dark to see her.

On mornings that I would walk, I would pray. Not just for Clovis, but for all my needs. I usually don't listen to music when I run as I love just running in the early morning darkness with all the peace that it brings. Stars still out, not many people out and about yet, and the only things wandering around other than an occasional fellow walker or runner would be the skunks. When I ran, I just ran, enjoying my time alone. On my walks, I would enjoy using my ear pods to listen to music. In the early morning hours, I would put on praise and worship music and sing along. Luckily for me (and my neighbors), no one else was around to hear me.

During this time, I would think, pray, and plan my day. It was the time the Lord would speak to me. As I walked, listening to my favorite songs, the one that came on over and over was "Reckless Love" by Cory Asbury. In this song, we hear about the shepherd who has 100 sheep. One of them goes missing, and the shepherd leaves the 99 to find the missing one. Jesus tells us this parable in Matthew 18:12-14.

"What do you think? If a man has a hundred sheep, and one of them has gone astray, does he not leave the ninety-nine and go to the mountains to seek the one that is straying? And if he should find it, assuredly, I say to you, he rejoices more over that sheep than over the ninety-nine that did not go astray." The song addresses this and shows us the love God has for us and the extent to which He will go to find us.

Before I spoke a word, You were singing over me
You have been so, so good to me.
Before I took a breath, You breathed Your life in me.
You have been so, so kind to me.

Oh, the overwhelming, never-ending, reckless love of God.
Oh, it chases me down, fights 'til I'm found, leaves the ninety-nine.
I couldn't earn it, and I don't deserve it, still, You give Yourself away.
Oh, the overwhelming, never-ending, reckless love of God.

When I was Your foe, still Your love fought for me.
You have been so, so good to me.
When I felt no worth, You paid it all for me
You have been so, so kind to me.

Oh, the overwhelming, never-ending, reckless love of God.
Oh, it chases me down, fights 'til I'm found, leaves the ninety-nine.
I couldn't earn it, and I don't deserve it, still You give Yourself away.
Oh, the overwhelming, never-ending, reckless love of God.

There's no shadow you won't light up
Mountain you won't climb up coming after me.
There's no wall You won't kick down
Lie You won't tear down Coming after me.

Yes, this was for my daughter. This was for me.

I needed to know that He was going to do whatever it takes to get his sheep to come home. As I walked, listened, and prayed, tears streaming down my face, I felt God was letting me know that everything would be OK. "I've got this!" He would tell me. "Stop worrying and lay it at my feet. Yes, she is your child, but she is also MY child. And I can do far more than you can ever ask, think or imagine." And in those moments, I would feel relief. A huge weight felt lifted from my shoulders. The burden I was carrying for Natalie was not mine but God's. Of course, over the months, I would take it back time and time again only to be reminded that He was the one that was ultimately going to reach her. Not me.

Of course, this song was not just for Natalie and me. It was for Clovis! Patty's comment to me made me realize that I had to continue to go after Clovis, just as God continues to go after people. I had developed such a love for this dog, which was crazy as I had never even thought about having a dog. The love I had for her was overwhelming and never-ending, it seemed. And yes, I felt like I would have climbed any mountain or broken down any walls to get to her. God was starting to show me just how much He loves us. If I could feel this much emotion over a stray dog, I couldn't even imagine how God must feel about His creation. I began to think about the day I might get to pet Clovis.

How exciting and thrilling that would be! The Bible says, "I say to you that likewise there will be more joy in heaven over one sinner who repents than over ninety-nine just persons who need no repentance." (Luke 15:7) Was God trying to show me through Clovis just how joyous He is over people?

If I could feel so much love for a dog, God must certainly feel 100 times that for Natalie—and for me! I was beginning to see that this wasn't just about Natalie anymore, but about all people. A love for people is what the Lord wanted to instill in my heart. And He was doing it all while I was out for a walk.

These morning walks were what I needed. It wasn't just the physical exercise that I needed—it was the mental and spiritual conditioning I needed. While I was walking, I was still looking for Clovis. Always looking.

Chapter 6

"Therefore, as the elect of God, holy and beloved, put on tender mercies, kindness, humility, meekness, longsuffering . . . ."
Colossians 3:12

As I continued to look for her, I reminded myself of the love that God has for us. He would never give up on us, and I couldn't give up on Clovis. God was not just developing a love and compassion in me for Clovis, but for all people. People will say, "I love all men equally," and I'm sure they say it with conviction, believing they mean it. I know I certainly have. But now, I was seeing just how shallow my love for other people could sometimes be.

Would I go after a person in need the way I was going after Clovis? Would I meet people's needs the way I was trying to meet Clovis' needs? That's how the Lord wants us to love. And not just those we like, agree with or are similar to. ALL people. People of every race. People of every sexual orientation. People of all political views. People who we find easy to love and those who are more difficult.

Every time we look into the eyes of another person, we are looking at someone that God loves! We may not feel that way about them, but God does. No matter who they are, what they believe, or what they have done, God still loves them. This was beginning to sink in deeply. At a time in our nation when people are being tugged apart and divided by race, religion, and politics, God is wanting us to pull together. To help one another. To truly love one another just as He loves us all. Regardless of the way we may think or feel, we are to love others the way God thinks and feels.   I was treating this dog how I was supposed to treat others. I realize that might sound simple. Something I should have known before. Sometimes it's these simple truths that suddenly hit us hard. I thought I knew what it meant to love others, to be compassionate and gentle. But now, it went so much deeper. And all because of a stray dog who was eluding me.

Every day, this lesson began to be ingrained in my mind. The patience and compassion I was showing Clovis were the same patience and compassion I needed for the people I see every day. The people that God brings across my path. The people that live in my neighborhood or shop at the same grocery store that I use. My eyes were opening up to the opportunities He places in front of us every day.

Opportunities ranging from giving a neighbor a ride to the doctor to helping a stranger that works at the grocery store with her rent one month. Everywhere I looked, I began to see people in need and those hurting.

People were still hurting from the effects of the Covid-19 pandemic. Many people were still not working enough to be able to pay their bills, and others were being overworked due to a lack of employees at places like grocery stores, restaurants, or other essential businesses. It was as if God was showing me people on a daily basis that needed help. His help. My help. After all, God uses people to help other people. It's one thing to say "I'll pray for you" to the hurting neighbor whose car is broken down and he can't get to work. It's quite another thing to say, "Here, borrow my car until yours is fixed." God was reinforcing in me the idea that we need to not only pray for people who are hurting, but we need to be the answer to those prayers when we can.

James 2:15-16 directly points this out:

> *"If a brother or sister is naked and destitute of daily food,*
> *and one of you says to them, 'Depart in peace,*
> *be warmed and filled,' but you do not give them the things*
> *which are needed for the body, what does it profit?"*

I was being taught to take action. Just like I was taking action to look for and help Clovis, I needed to start taking action to help people. For now, I wanted to keep my main focus on Clovis as she was the reason this was all happening. She was the purpose of my life at the moment. However, while I was trying to rescue her, I began looking for ways to help people as well. Clovis had given me this new purpose—a purpose that would be tested now and then when I wouldn't see her for days.

I would see Clovis in certain spots most days, but then she would vanish for a day or two. Where could she go? I would so worry that something had happened to her. If I didn't see her for a day, I assumed I just missed her. On those rare occasions when she would vanish for three or four days, I assumed the worst. I would practically be wringing my hands, pacing around with worry. Then, one night, she would show back up on the game camera. I would find such relief upon seeing her sneak up at night to get her food and then realize I had worried for nothing. I tried not to fret too much. She had survived the harsh winter, but my mind would wander to all the "what ifs." I always wondered where she hid for several days at a time and would most likely never know. Happy to see her return, I would again stick to my routine.

After my morning run, I would always take my handkerchief over to the blanket I had laid out for her. I always tucked one into my shorts as I ran or walked. I learned this trick from one of my older sisters, Laurie, who also runs. She lives in Bartlesville, Oklahoma, the town I grew up in and started my running adventures. The handkerchief is great for sweat in the summer and runny noses in the winter.

And now it was good for attracting a dog. I knew my scent was all over that handkerchief. What harm could come of me setting it out every morning where I put her breakfast? I wanted her to associate the food and treats with my scent.

I was running or walking from my home every morning. No more was I going to my running club in Grapevine. I wanted to, but it would break my routine. I wanted Clovis to know when I was coming. I wanted her to grow dependent on the times that I would bring her food or treats. I couldn't miss a day. She needed to be able to trust in me and rely on my faithfulness to her. It was difficult not to see my running friends on the weekends, but after 2020, when so much was shut down due to Covid-19, many people were still not back to their normal routines. Many of our friends assumed Randy and I were trying to stay away from crowds to stay safe and healthy. In reality, we were staying away to show Clovis our devotion and faithfulness to her. I didn't ever reach out to anyone at the running club about our absence, mainly because I assumed no one would understand. After all, how could a stray dog be so hard to catch? How could a stray dog need so much attention? Yes, they were all my friends, but none of them had seen Clovis or been around her.

I don't think anyone who wasn't in our neighborhood could understand the conditions Clovis was living in or the effort it was taking to catch her. Randy and I ran from home the entire year, never visiting with our friends at LGRAW. Hopefully, it would pay off for us in the end. Maybe one day, Clovis might go to the running club with us and run on the trails! That was a dream in my mind. The paw would have to be looked at first. For now, however, I just needed to stay focused on being here for her. I was afraid that even one morning of not showing up for her on time might cause her to lose trust in me. Was I ever going to be able to be gone and leave her?

In June, this fear was tested. We went to Montana for a week to visit family. All I could think of was getting back to Clovis. Here we are in one of the most beautiful places in the United States, near Glacier National Park, and I'm longing to get home because of a dog. We had a wonderful time in Montana and my sisters got to hear the entire story of Clovis. Randy and I would talk about her daily, wondering if she was OK. I was enjoying my family time, no doubt. But I also had this pit-like feeling in my stomach, and Randy knew it. He would ask me what I was thinking about, knowing that my mind was on Clovis. Of course, his was too. I felt as though I had left a young child at home alone, fending for herself for a week. But she wasn't completely alone. I had left my daughter, Sydney, in charge of feeding her with detailed instructions of what to do:

FEED CLOVIS!

"I realize she is a stray, but I have been working hard to gain her trust, so I need her to be kept on the schedule. Here's what I want you to do:

"Every morning, she gets dry food (about half full in the green bowl) and ½ can of her wet food mixed in. Please put it out between 6-7 am as that is when she comes through on her route through the woods. Just place it inside the opening of the fence.

"Sometimes she drags it further into the woods, and you might have to get a long stick to pull it back to you. Or you might have to go into the woods from the backside and brave the thorns!

"If she hasn't eaten it by about 10 am, she missed it and won't be by. Be sure to go back and pick it up! There is also a water container by where I put her food. You might take a large bottle/cup of freshwater to change it out. It's not AS necessary as I think she gets water at the creek.

"Every evening, she comes by between 9:30-10. The raccoons usually get to it by then. So please give her the same amount of food in the green bowl and put it out on the blanket outside the kitchen window. Place one of her kabob treats on the blanket next to it. I also turn all the kitchen/dining lights out, EXCEPT the one over the sink. This helps keep the raccoons away as it shines out on the blanket. Clovis can see the food from the street.

"You'll know the next morning if it was her that got it because she drags the bowl away from the blanket and licks it clean. Please give her fresh water every day, too, even if it's full. Please dump it and fill it with the hose.

"I would appreciate it if you would call her name when you put it out too. I think she knows it now---at least she hears me say it all the time, and I think she equates it to mealtime.

"Her dry food is in the utility room in the bucket.
Her wet food and treats are under the kitchen sink. I know I have gone on and on about this, but this is very important. I know it means you have to get up extra early, but it's all I ask of you."

I explained where she was to put the food and at what times. I had tried to explain to Sydney about the raccoons, but I also realized she didn't have the time or the desire to sit outside for hours on end and chase them away every night as I had been doing. I knew she didn't have the same fervor for getting Clovis, so I told myself I would be happy if she would just put food and water out.

Don't check the camera. Don't put clothing out. Don't walk and look for her. Please just feed her on time. And she did. I called or texted Sydney every day, asking if she had seen Clovis. The answer was usually a resounding "No." My heart was hurting, and I was getting worried. Maybe Sydney wasn't seeing her because of the time of day that Clovis would come? Maybe Clovis was only coming in the middle of the night, and with the camera not set up, Sydney would miss her? Or maybe, Clovis knew I was gone and because the routine had been broken, she went another direction. I was concerned and couldn't wait to get back home to check on her.

When I returned a week later, Clovis had vanished. It would be almost two weeks before I would see her again. Randy will tell you that I was a wreck for those two weeks. A miserable, crying, worrying wreck. I walked the neighborhoods looking for her every chance I got. I hopped on my bike every day, knowing I could cover more ground in a short amount of time than by foot. I rode up and down every street around our neighborhood, looking for her, binoculars hanging around my neck just in case I needed them.

I checked the camera every night and still took food to her usual spots every morning and night. Most of the time, the food would be gobbled up by raccoons or left untouched if I had left it across the street by the bamboo plants. I would head back inside, with my head down, wondering if something had happened to her. I didn't think she would run far away at this point, but I had no idea where she might be. Had she been hit by a car? Had she gotten in a tussle with a pack of coyotes? I looked for her on my walks and continued to set up the game camera, hoping to catch a glimpse of her at night, but I saw nothing for several days. Only raccoons.

I began to worry about her, but then one morning, there she was on the game camera. She had finally come back! I was overjoyed! I couldn't wait to run to tell Randy. "She's alive! She's back!!"I'm convinced she was gone because the schedule was interrupted. I truly felt like it was all my fault for leaving her during that time. I vowed not to leave again until we caught her. I needed to be reliable. She needed to know she could trust that I would be there. Always.

As much as I wanted Clovis to learn to trust me, I also knew that many other people were looking out for her, seeing her on their walks or their drives to work. Most people who saw her assumed, as I did at first, that she was someone's dog that got loose. After a few sightings, they would also begin to wonder. Around the first week of July, I saw another post on *Nextdoor* concerning Clovis:

6 Jul
Amber G, Lonesome Dove Estates
Dog. For the last two weeks, I have seen this dog limping around. It is at Lonesome Dove and Foxfire, living around the construction. I've been feeding and giving water the whole time, but it is so scared and runs away. I have called animal control 2-3 times to help, but nothing has come of it, from what I can tell. I know it's not a great picture, but it is brown and black. Looks like a German Shepherd mix? Does anyone recognize or have you seen posts about a missing dog? It is hurt and scared and so hard to catch. Southlake, TX

Stacie, Southlake
Amber, this dog has been around for at least two years, and I've been trying desperately to win her over (yes, it's a girl—my game camera caught a clear shot!). I feed her twice a day and fresh water too. Animal control has been out before, as have the police, but she has not been caught. At this point, they said to leave her alone because if they try to catch her and she bites them, they will have to put her down. We are on top of it, and I watch for her every day. If you try to catch her, she's only going to run and be even more scared. I'm trying to win her over and let her come to me on her terms. Just know that she is being taken care of as much as possible. Even the police and animal control could not get her. She comes over to our house in the evenings but won't let me get near. I'm hoping with time that she will come around! We have named her Clovis. The name means one who fights to survive. And she lived through that snowstorm we had back in February. We had blankets and straw out for her to sleep in, but she still wouldn't come close to us. She somehow managed to live through that though! My fingers are crossed that I can win her over eventually. We live in the first house on foxfire (the small white one), so we can easily keep up with her.

Amber G, Lonesome Dove Estates
Thank you for sharing all of this information. That's the same doggie! I just recently have been seeing her but didn't know she has been around for the last two years!! I'm glad she's being fed by you as well bc I got worried when I was out of town this past weekend. I even had my sister go fill up the bowls.

Stacie, Southlake
My husband tells our friends that we now have a dog. :-) I want her so badly!! I try everything to get her without scaring her. I think it will just take time and her learning to trust us.

Rhonda K, Southlake
God bless you, Stacie, for your efforts!
How often do you see her? Does she come around every day?

Stacie, Southlake
Yes/—every morning and every evening

Karla S, Winding Creek Estates
God Bless you for watching out for her.

Tonya D, Trophy Club
Thanks for helping her survive all of this time! Clovis is a beautiful dog and name.

Stacie, Southlake
In our front yard one night (I posted her picture).

Rhonda K, Southlake
Clovis is a beautiful girl - praying for a breakthrough, and she comes to you!

Diane B, Hidden Lake Estates
You can try contacting Duck Team 6. They are a volunteer group that captures street dogs.

Robby R, Southlake
The dog has been around for over a year, maybe two years. I am not aware of him ever hurting anyone or anything. And yes, he is very skittish. One of the neighbors called SL police, and they came out. They are aware of the dog and said they tried to catch him about a year ago without any luck. They had three police cars and 4-5 officers and still didn't catch him. Quite a few people put food and water out for him.

Amber G, Lonesome Dove Estates
I just don't know how I am just now seeing the dog!

Stacie, Southlake
The lot that she hangs out in used to be 2 acres of woods and only one house. She had plenty of coverage! Now it has been plowed down, and homes were going up there, so her "home" is diminishing. However, she seems to like Robby's house (see above post), and she frequents mine as well. We have about 5 acres of wooded land around us that she also hides/hangs out in. You are probably seeing her more now due to the construction that is going on, causing her to have to find other places to hang out.

Darren C, Trophy Club
I used to be heavily involved in dog rescue. When we moved to Texas 20 years ago, there were many stray dogs. Sometimes they get loose right when people move here, as a dog can find an escape point in a wooden privacy fence very quickly. I've noticed a large increase in normal lost dogs with the influx of population

here. Dogs like this one are the hardest to catch. I'll say right now that the lack of training for police officers to catch them is zero. Plus, there are miles and miles between Animal Control Officers. I got to know the Officer for Trophy Club over our first five years. When he retired, I don't think he was ever replaced. I'm sure things have improved at the animal shelters, but they used to be the LAST place you'd take a stray dog. Over in Wise County, they were still hooking up a hose to a pickup truck exhaust and running it into the pound to "euthanize" animals. Things are even worse for sick or injured dogs. There's budget for vet care. Used to be, it a new doggie prisoner came in and tested for Parvo, the pounds would kill every dog in there. True. It is very rare for a stray like this one to have been around for years. Has anyone been able to guess an age? Or, male or female? How about a weight estimate? The limping is not a good sign. That means if there is somewhere the dog goes at night where there's sort of an "owner," they are being negligent. It's always bothered me that people seem to catch all kinds of wildlife when they put their mind to it. In a case like this one, a large trap with all of the food in it and checked at least three times a day would be the way to go. Some Feed Stores have them. It's a huge undertaking, and the dog's not going to be in a great mood if injured. He'll need several people to work together to get him to a safe location—and that trap will be HEAVY. And then there's going to have to be several vet trips. One of the many reasons dogs are the best thing ever is that no matter how mean or injured, they will respond quickly to a human-provided safe environment. They are wired to do that. After the dog is healed and calm and one can determine the age and temperament, that's when you find a foster home. God, I don't know what I'd do if a coyote was sitting in the trap one morning! Panic, I guess.

Stacie, Southlake
And that is the issue here ... I have Clovis (the dog) and coyotes on camera together at night. And this dog is SMART. When it was snowing, we rigged a shelter for her, but she wouldn't go near it .... she realized it was new and she wouldn't have anything to do with it. I know it sounds crazy, but I don't think she would EVER go into a trap... it's like she knows! I see her several times a day, feed her, talk to her all the time, so she gets used to me. I've even put a shirt out by where she sleeps so she would get used to our scent. Crazy, I know, but I'm trying everything! :-)

Robert W, N Southlake
The trap is a great idea if you put some good cooked meat in there! But as you say correctly, that is just the beginning ... after

tons of vet bills and a lot of work you still don't know how fast she will improve. It looks like she was abused before, and that can take a while.

Rhonda K, Southlake
I wish I never read your comment Darren, my imagination is vivid, and what Wise County used to do... I'm very upset!

Lynn M, Southlake
I would donate $ to get her vetted and spayed, etc. I'm sure other animal lovers would also donate to help her. It sounds like she will already have a good home once Stacy can catch her. Lol. Thanks to everyone for trying to help Clovis.

Amber G, Lonesome Dove Estates
I would help out financially to get her cleaned up as well!

Stacie, Southlake
You all are so sweet and generous! If I am successful, I will let you all know, of course. This could take months, but I'm being patient and trying to let her eventually come to me. Any attempt to go towards her just scares her more. She has come a few times after dark to eat in my front yard while I sat on the porch about 15 yards away. So that's a start! She has to have been an abused dog ... I've never seen a dog this scared before, especially after feeding her all these months. The deer, coyotes, and raccoons in my backyard are not as scared of me as she is!

7 Jul
Tonya D, Trophy Club
I'd also contribute. Please let me know when she's caught ...

Sabrina G, Kimberly Estates
Stacie - you've got it covered, and thank you for your kind and caring soul.

Cyndia M, Winding Creek Estates
Stacy, I recommend that you call DuckTeam as well. They know everything about capturing dogs. I'm sure they could give you some useful tips.

What an awesome neighborhood and city! So many strangers reaching out for the sake of this sweet dog. I couldn't believe how many people volunteered to help with her veterinarian bills! And all the tips and advice were greatly appreciated. I did consider calling the Duck Team that people mentioned, but then again, even thinking about a team of people coming out to capture her, as they do "street dogs," made me cringe. Once again, I didn't want to trap Clovis. She was going to trap us. I understood it would take longer, but I also believed it was the best way to go. After all, we were the ones watching her every day, seeing her disposition, her intelligence, her behavior. Several of us in the neighborhood agreed that going slower, being caring, and showing patience was the best method for this particular dog.

At this point, I was still putting meals out in my front yard. She was way too smart to come by in the daylight. It was either before dawn or after dark that she made her rounds. And then the camera caught it: one evening, she came by, grabbed her treat AND the handkerchief, and ran off. Did she mean to take it? Was this her way of letting me know she knew it was me? I wasn't sure. But then it happened again and again. I would find them lying by her bed or behind the rock pile where she would run to eat her treats. She was taking them on purpose! From that moment on, I always laid one out by her food with a treat on top. I wanted her to know it was me bringing her the treats. After a few weeks, however, I realized that I was now missing some of my handkerchiefs. She took so many that I never found some of them. Thankfully, the store sells inexpensive ones in a 12-pack for a few dollars. I had a feeling I might need quite a few more in the upcoming weeks.

Robby and I had discussed at one time how Clovis wouldn't look at us. Just as wild animals feel threatened when we stare directly at them, Clovis seemed to feel the same way. Robby once told me, "Stacie, Clovis could be lying in our back yard, far away from our patio, just lying in the grass. I could be at my grill, cooking dinner, going in and out, and she would just lie there. If I looked right at her and she saw me, she would take off. Sometimes, she would merely run off to lie behind some bushes where she felt hidden, as though I didn't know she was there. Something about looking directly at her made her run."

Yes, she did that to me as well.

All this time, day after day, Clovis wouldn't look right at me. If she did, she would bolt! She could see me coming with her food and trot off a bit, but if I looked right at her, she would run. I learned early on to talk to her, all while trying not to look too much at her. I wanted to, though! I wanted to see her cute face and try to have eye contact with her. I suppose it was just too much for her. I would have to bide my time and do what I could. I continued to talk to Clovis daily, trying not to intimidate her with my stare.

One day, after six months of our same routine, I noticed something: Surprisingly, Clovis was not running as wildly as she had before. Nor was she avoiding all eye contact with me! She would watch for me coming with her food. Even though she would trot off, she would look at me from a distance while I spoke to her. However, she was only running 20-30 yards away and waiting. Waiting for me to leave her food. I had gone back to feeding her breakfast across the street again.

She was always missing the food in the mornings at my house due to other hungry critters. I decided it was more important for her to get to eat than to get her in my yard. When I took her food over, she would see me, jaunt off a bit and out of sight, and wait. Sometimes, I could see her waiting; she would hide just out of my sight. I knew she was still there. She wanted her meal. She just didn't want it badly enough to come get it from me. Why? I would have thought that most strays would have ventured toward me by now. Maybe they wouldn't come to get a treat from my hand, but they would have at least tried to come closer. Even those raccoons came closer than Clovis! She must have been hurt terribly to have such distrust for humans.

It had now been about six months since we began this pursuit, and Clovis now had her own personal food delivery service. I sat the food down, turned to walk back home, and by the time I got back across the street to my house, she was there eating. I would holler back to her, "Clovis, good girl! I'm so glad you got your food! I hope you have a great day today, Clovis!" She would look right at me, staring from across the street. THIS WAS PROGRESS! The progress wasn't as fast as I wanted, but when is anything the Lord does ever on our timeline? I was so excited! I ran in to tell Randy, but I'm not quite sure that even he understood the significance for me. As I did most days, I grabbed the binoculars and watched her eat from our bedroom window, which was at the front of our house. I'm not sure what I thought was going to happen. I just wanted to see what she did next. Where would she go? Sometimes she would run off when she finished. Sometimes, she would lay down by the food and blanket and rest a bit. I felt like something was beginning to happen. Were kindness, compassion, and patience finally starting to pay off? I was hopeful!

Chapter 7

"My sheep hear My voice, and I know them, and they follow Me."
John 10:27

Now that I was feeling a bit more hopeful, I was looking for more signs, more progress. Maybe I shouldn't have because it would often be days, even weeks before I would notice something new. That was so discouraging. I was putting in so much time and effort and felt no reward. After everything I was doing, she still wouldn't come to me.

It was now late summer, the hottest days in Texas, and I finally discovered that she was spending a lot of time in Robby's backyard during the day. I had noticed that she tended to run in the direction of his house, plus Robby had mentioned that he had been feeding her during the snowstorm, so I ventured that way to see if she was there. Surprise surprise! Curled up in the far corner of his backyard, there she was. I knew that she liked that area, and I would see her now and then, but I didn't realize how much time she was sleeping there. In that far corner of his lot was an old playhouse from years ago. The upper platform yielded shade underneath for Clovis.

She would lie there during our 90 to 100-degree days, trying to stay out of the scorching Texas sun. Because the area under the playhouse did not get mowed as often as the rest of Robby's yard, the high grass provided a nice hiding spot for Clovis. When she was lying down, she was very hard to detect. If you had not seen her there before, you would have never noticed this 65-pound animal sleeping soundly. This north side of Robby's yard was adjacent to Tim and Julie's yard.

This side was fenced off with a six-foot wooden privacy fence. About two-thirds the way down the privacy fence, a chain-link fence began. This chain-link fence left about a one-foot gap at the end, not quite reaching the end of the property line. Clovis liked that she could get out of Robby's yard and into Tim and Julie's through that gap. I liked that I could leave a treat for her right in that opening.

I began walking over to the fence every day by way of Tim and Julie's front yard, several times a day, to take her a treat and talk to her. On many occasions, Clovis would be lying in Tim and Julie's front yard, sacked out under the large oak trees, trying to get relief from the hot Texas summer sun. They had placed a couple of large buckets of water out for her and would change it out regularly. She had shade and water. I worried that the heat was still too much for her, even though we were having a mild summer in comparison to other years. She slept a lot in the heat. She slept so still that we all often wondered if she was OK. If she was even still alive. She must have felt safe in their vast yard with plenty of acreage to run if danger approached. It was relatively quiet in their yard and not right next to the busy road. Sometimes, to cool herself, Clovis would lie behind the bushes on the side of their home, right up against the house. She was hidden. I saw her one day and thought, "I wonder how many times I have missed her there? How long has that been her hiding spot?" Tim and Julie were quite lucky, I thought!

They could sit inside their home and watch her. They had great views of our baby girl. One afternoon, I received a text from Julie: "I think Clovis is part Ridgeback. If you look up Ridgeback dogs, you'll see the long ridge of fur that grows in the opposite direction down their backs. Clovis has that ridge going down her spine." I wasn't sure because I didn't have as good a view as Julie did, but I looked up the pictures online, and she seemed to be on the right track.

Clovis looked like she was part Ridgeback. Ridgeback mixed with German Shepherd? The pictures of this mix of breeds were almost Clovis exactly. She had the body shape and ears of the Ridgeback but the coloring of the German Shepherd. She might even have a little hound dog in her too!

Whenever I would walk over to Tim and Julie's yard to find Clovis, I was expecting her to be either in their front yard or in Robby's back yard. I would sneak up as quietly as I could, trying to get as close as possible so as not to scare her. A few times, I got within about 20 feet, but she would eventually see me and jump up, run through the gap in the fence, and head to Robby's. She felt protected behind the fence. I could have easily slipped through the gap myself, but why chase her? She would have only run further. I would stand in my usual spot at the fence, coaxing her to me, waving a chicken jerky treat at her.

One day, while approaching, I realized that she wasn't running as far away anymore. She would still trot off a few steps as though she might flee, but it wasn't with the same fear as she had before. I would stand at the fence and talk to her. I wanted her to get used to my voice. I wanted her to KNOW my voice. I'm not even sure what I would say. I would chit chat with her about anything as if she knew what I was saying.

"Good morning, Clovis! You're such a sweet girl. How are you today? I hope you're staying out of the hot sun. If you would just come over to my house, I could keep you cool in the summer and warm in the winter!" I would often ramble about anything.

I would tell her what I was doing that day, how my favorite sports team was doing, how the new house construction was progressing—anything to talk to her.   I'm quite certain as cars drove by and saw me standing there talking to no one, they thought I was nuts. I didn't care. All I was focused on was Clovis. After chatting with her about anything I could think of, I would lay my handkerchief down on the ground near the opening of the fence and place a treat on top. She would lay across the yard, watching me, but never near. "At least she isn't running anymore," I would think to myself! As I walked away from the fence and through Tim and Julie's yard and back to the street, I would look back to watch. After a few seconds, I could see her run to get the treat. She knew exactly what I was doing by placing the handkerchief down. She had learned there would be a treat waiting for her and that I was the one brining it. She knew she could count on me, but she didn't know me well enough to trust me completely yet.

This continued every day, four to five times a day. Because I work from home, I would take every break I had, whether 15 minutes or an hour, to find her and take her a treat. I was almost afraid I was feeding her too much, but then again, could I feed a dog who is out on her own all the time too much? I asked our neighborhood veterinarian and fellow runner, Beverly Unger-Zipfel, about showering Clovis with treats. She said there was no way I could give her too many right now.

I needed to reward her every chance I got. Winning her heart through food. I like it!

I have always teased that is how I won Randy's heart. Now was my opportunity to reach Clovis' heart through treats.

 When a client would leave my house, I would walk over to find Clovis and talk to her, give her a treat, then get back home in time for the next client. If someone had to cancel a training session, I was almost elated. Not because I didn't want to train my client or do my job, but because it meant I had more time to dedicate to Clovis.

I kept up with my routine, but I was also racking my brain to think of other ways to win this dog over.

I had lots of advice from well-meaning people because I had never had a dog. I was winging it. I was doing what I thought would work. And so, others felt compelled to give me tips.

One neighbor asked, "Have you tried clapping your hands and saying 'come here, girl'?"

A client asked, "Have you tried giving her a treat?"

Others would say, "If you just take some yummy treats or some slices of meat and leave a trail, she will come right to you!"

I could have hung a raw steak around my neck, and Clovis would not have budged an inch towards me. As much as she might want that food, she knew better. I was at times only 15 yards away, turkey or ham in my hand, and Clovis would lie there, staring at me, not moving or flinching.

I know she wanted it, but she wasn't about to budge. The minute I set it down on the handkerchief and walked away, she would run and snatch it up. I think I mentioned she was smart. The tips didn't end there.

"Have you tried a trap? They have these large traps that you can set up, and when they go in them to get the food, the door shuts on them." Yes, we had thought of those. But she wouldn't go into anything, and again, what would I do with her then? If I did trap her, she would be so scared that all my efforts would have been in vain. Whenever I thought of using a trap, I envisioned Clovis, inside, trapped and scared, looking at me as if to say, "What are you doing to me? I thought you were going to be my friend!"

No, I couldn't fathom using a trap.

"Have you tried snapping your fingers and saying, 'Here, girl'?" "Uh, gee, I guess I hadn't thought of that."

"You need to call this rescue squad. It's a team of people that come out and trap stray dogs."

For goodness sakes, no! The last thing I needed at this point was for Clovis to feel even more scared or less trusting. We were making progress, and I wasn't about to go backward with an entire group of strangers coming after her! Besides, she wasn't hurting anyone or anything and certainly wasn't a threat.

Another neighbor driving by saw Clovis in the field and stopped to ask me about her. I briefly told her she was a stray, and she replied, "I'll go home and get a leash and send my boys down to get her." "Go right ahead. I would like to see that happen," I thought to myself.

Others would advise, "Stacie, if you just start moving her food bowl a few feet closer to your front door every night, she will eventually come to your porch!" "Um, no. She won't," I thought. This is no ordinary dog. She isn't just a stray who has been lost for a few days. She has been out there for almost THREE YEARS. She knows better. She wasn't going to do anything that she felt would put her in danger or a confined space. This is how she survived and kept herself safe from people and cars.

This dog would sit at the edge of the road and look both ways before crossing! I watched her on multiple occasions, and she was smarter than most humans I have seen crossing a street. She would look, and if a car was coming from one direction, she would back up, lie down, and wait. It truly was amazing to watch. Clovis was smart! The ordinary tricks that would usually work for strays would not work for Clovis. I had figured that out.

It wasn't just people we knew who commented about Clovis. Week after week, cars would stop on one of the roads around the domain that Clovis was covering and inquire about her as they would see her running through the woods, crossing streets, and limping through ditches along the roads. I would tell them the same story and let them know we were working on getting her. No one could believe that she was that uncatchable, especially with an injured paw. Again, how could they know?

They couldn't know. They hadn't been watching her every day for months like I had. It was very encouraging to know that so many neighbors cared about Clovis. They cared enough to stop and try to get her. And I had to keep telling myself that. My first thought would be, "Stop! You're going to ruin everything!" But all would be fine, and it was just an opportunity for me to see what a great community of people Randy and I live among.

I knew that everyone was very well-meaning with their tips and advice. Of course, they just wanted to help. But it was painfully obvious to me that people didn't understand. How could they?

Most people they knew who had rescued a dog went to a shelter and adopted one. Some potential pet owners look online, using sites like Petfinder, to see what animals are available for adoption. These are great resources and a fantastic way to save an animal that might not otherwise find a home. I even have a friend who pulled into a shopping center, opened her car door, and a stray jumped into her lap. What a great story! But this was not an ordinary rescue situation. Clovis was, in essence, a wild dog. Not aggressive but wild. She wasn't going to jump into our laps. No one was ever going to drive up, hop out of their car, wave food in front of her, and have her come running to them. She was going to have to know us. She was going to have to recognize us. Recognize our voices. Recognize our love for her. And so, we kept on.

Randy was probably getting so tired of hearing me talk about this dog. I would come in every single day with the latest news on Clovis. Grabbing the binoculars and shouting, "Look! There she is!" was probably getting tiring to him. But, supportive as always, he was right there with me, doing anything I asked of him. Whether it was going to buy dog food, helping me set up a tarp over her bed during the rain and hail storms, or simply allowing me to take whatever time I needed to spend with Clovis, he was there. One summer day during a hard rain, with hail on its way, we tried to set up a tarp over her straw bed.

Out in the rain, Randy was pounding in stakes and rigging up a blue plastic tarp, leaving it open on three sides so that Clovis could see and not feel trapped. I was feeling so relieved that Clovis would have coverage from the storm. It almost made me feel heroic for giving her this makeshift shelter. But she never used it. Once she saw the tarp, a signal went off in her head—TRAP! RUN! After two days, Randy took the tarp down. We realized it only made her even more cautious if not outright suspicious. Clovis returned to her bedding once the tarp was gone. Later we would learn that Clovis had other ways of protecting herself during storms. She would burrow underneath brush, dig deep holes in the ground where she would lie, and of course, I'm sure she had numerous other tricks that we never discovered. Randy's tarp was just not something she wanted to chance. But thank you, Randy! I always knew I could count on him.

As my daily visits to Robby's yard continued into September, Randy started coming with me some of the time. We both talked to Clovis and took her treats. She was getting spoiled for a stray! And hopefully, she was getting used to hearing us and learning my voice. It would take at least another month or two before I saw more progress. But for now, I was satisfied that she wasn't running as much. She was even starting to look right at us for longer periods from a shorter distance. Those piercing brown eyes, now staring into mine from a distance, told me that she was beginning to come around. This was progress.

Chapter 8

"Wait on the Lord; be of good courage, and He shall strengthen your heart; Wait, I say, on the Lord!"

Psalm 27:14

As I was starting to be encouraged by what little progress I saw, I was also disappointed as I wanted things to move faster. Always faster. I was ready to get this little doggie and give her hugs and kisses. She just wasn't ready. Would she ever be ready? She was still eating her breakfast across the street, and I would continue to pick her up on my game camera in our yard at night. But why wouldn't she stay? Our house seemed the perfect place to me. No neighbors on either side. No construction sites. 5 acres of fields and trees. It seemed like a dog's heaven! Yet she remained across the street or over at Robby's. I was getting impatient and tired of waiting.

One morning, I woke up to once again find the food bowl gone. That silly girl! Where has she taken it? I looked everywhere for it. The yard, the field, the lot across the street. Where was it? I finally decided it was gone for good. Maybe the wind picked it up since it was just a lightweight plastic container. I got another one and continued the pattern.

About a week later, while talking to Clovis by the fence at Robby's house, I noticed something in the tall grass. There was my bowl! Clovis had carried her dinner about 200 meters and across two streets to Robby's yard. She was a tricky little girl. I could only envision what she must have looked like, carrying a green plastic bowl in her mouth, limping all the way. At least I knew where it had gone!

I thought that was the end of the mystery once I found that bowl. But no. It happened repeatedly, and I could never find them. I was now missing three or four dishes that I had put out in our front yard at night. The game camera would prove once again to help me out.

There on the camera, I saw the culprit. It wasn't Clovis this time. The coyote was coming into the front yard and snatching up her dinner and slinking off with it. I decided it was time to upgrade, so off to Petsmart I went. I found a decent-sized bowl, still made of plastic, but it was fairly heavy. I thought there would be no way a dog or a coyote would be able to carry this one-off.

One night in, I discovered I was wrong. The coyote, on camera once again, picked up the entire bowl with the food and ran off with it! I was now missing all kinds of dishes! I was surprised the coyote's jaw was able to hold that heavier one and run with it, but he did. It took me almost two months before I found my bowls. I had given up on ever using them again and finally gave in and bought a more expensive, heavy-duty porcelain dog food dish. Take that, you coyote! I'd like to see you carry that thing off! And let me tell you, he did try. On several occasions, the same coyote would attempt to grab it in his mouth to steal it, but it was just too heavy. A few weeks later, while walking out in the field behind my house, curiously looking everywhere for all my missing bowls, I decided to climb over the barbed wire fence that separates the property from the Corp of Engineers property.

Lying back in the woods were all my missing bowls. The coyote had not only stolen them, but run with them, jumped a fence with them, and left them all in one place. Poor Clovis. I had been blaming her for being a thief, wrongly accusing her based on the prior incidents. For all I knew, those two could have been in this together!

I joked about Clovis being in cahoots with the coyote, but in all honestly, I worried about her due to her limp. While she was a large dog, bigger than the coyotes, I would have thought the coyotes would have preyed on her, seeing that she might be in a weakened state. It still amazes me that Clovis was never attacked by the packs that live behind our house in the woods. Normally, they would leave a dog of her size alone, but did they view her as vulnerable?

Coyotes often get a bad rap from people who think they are out to get their animals. Coyotes are actually quite shy by nature, avoiding human contact when possible.

They aren't necessarily nocturnal either. Seeing one during the day doesn't mean he is rabid or sick. It might mean he is searching for food and feels unthreatened at that time. Coyotes typically chase after rodents, squirrels, or rabbits for their meals.

True, they may attack cats or small dogs, and you should keep an eye on your small pets if they are outdoors, but those are not their usual preferences. When coyotes do come around our home, loud yelling and vigorous clapping are enough to scare them away. Randy and I try to view coyotes as we do the other wildlife—animals to be respected and appreciated, just as we try to do all animals. Still, I worried about Clovis with her limp, yet almost three years later, she was unscathed.

She was unscathed, not just because she was smart, but she was also an escape artist! She could get herself out of any dangerous situation it seemed. Later, I would come to believe that God's protective hand was on this girl. She had made it through the snowstorm. She had survived racing cars on the roads. She had survived encounters with coyotes. And she seemed to be untouched. I knew that God's hand was on this girl.

I realize that for some, animals are just that—animals. But God created animals, and in Genesis 1, He said, "It is good." Even the book of Revelation says, "You are worthy, O Lord, to receive glory and honor and power; for You created all things, and by Your will, they exist and were created." (4:11). God created animals. Not just the ones we love, cuddle or feel comfortable with. All animals. Clovis, the deer, and even the coyotes. Animals show us over and over again how God loves us. When you see a lion protecting her cub, you see how God will also protect us. When you see a mama bird providing food for her newborn chicks, it reminds us how God will also provide for us. God wants us to care for His animals.

Just as He loves them and cares for them, He wants us to be a reflection of Him and love them as well. I knew God cared for Clovis, and I believed in time, He would bring her to me. He tells us in Psalm 145:9 that He cares about His animals and hears their cries: "The Lord is good to all, and His tender mercies are over all his works." Clovis was one of God's works! But Psalm 145 doesn't end there. Verses 15-17 say, "The eyes of all look expectantly to You, and You give them their food in due season. You open Your hand and satisfy the desire of every living thing." Clovis, like all animals, was an "every living thing."

I knew the Lord was watching out for Clovis and, at the moment, using me to try to reach her. I also knew that He wanted to satisfy the desire she had for warmth, food, affection, and a home. I just wanted to know when He would bring her to me. I wished I knew why it was taking so long. Isn't she getting just as tired of playing this game as I am?

Surely this isn't just to teach me more patience? I felt like I had been patient enough! How ironic.

Patience itself takes time to develop. Psalm 40:1-3 says, "I waited patiently for the Lord; He inclined to me and heard my cry. He also brought me up out of a horrible pit, out of the miry clay, and set my feet upon a rock, and established my steps." Boy, did I feel like I was in a miry clay pit some days with Clovis. A thick, slimy mud pit in which I was sinking. Here, Clovis is the one out in the weather all alone, day and night, night and day, yet I am the one feeling like I'm drowning in a pit. My emotions were starting to get the best of me. I guess God thought I needed a little more patience, and I had more lessons to be learned.

Learning these lessons on patience wasn't easy. I felt so discouraged that things weren't moving, yet I just had to keep trying. By late September, it seemed that Clovis had narrowed down her terrain. She hardly ever went missing anymore. I would see her every day. This was good. She felt like she was in a safe spot. Maybe she didn't feel the urgency to run away anymore. For whatever the reason, she was staying put around four homes. Randy and I saw issues coming, though, due to the construction. If Clovis didn't move toward me quicker, we might have a problem on our hands.

The last house across the street was going up, and the lot Clovis often hung out in was diminished. There was orange construction fencing up in areas to protect trees and prevent trash from blowing all over the place. Clovis had found refuge in these areas. I would find her sleeping in a small area of the construction site, full of weeds and trash. It saddened me to see her sleeping there, but she was very well hidden. If you didn't know she was there, you would walk right past her, which everyone did. She would also find relief from the summer sun on top of a giant sand pile on one of the building lots. White, fine sand piled about 5 feet high was one of her new napping places in the mornings.

I first saw her there while out on a walk early one morning, around 6:00 am. Sprawled out on top like a sunbather at the beach—she was enjoying the cool touch of that white sand. In Texas, the summer temperatures don't cool down at night like you might get in Colorado. The summer temperatures continue through September. Our daytime temperatures reach 100+ but the darkness of night may only bring those temperatures down to 80 if we are lucky. So even at 6:00 am, it's hot and humid, warmer than many states get during the heat of their day. The sand was a respite for Clovis. She never stayed there long, though, as construction workers would soon pull in by 7:00 am, and she would be on the move again. At least she was hanging around this immediate area now. We knew that a swimming pool would be going in and permanent fencing in a matter of weeks or months, but we didn't know when.

What we did know was that once those fences went up and that pool was dug, Clovis would not be able to cut through the fields to get to our house. We would have to work fast.

We no longer had a blanket for her in that area due to the construction and the workers. We would have to find a new place. In the meantime, she seemed to be doing OK, finding hiding spots.

We couldn't figure out why she wouldn't just cross the street and come to our house and yard. There was no construction on our side of the street, and we were surrounded by woods on all sides. It seemed a perfect place for a dog to hide and relax. But she knew what she was doing. Our only guess was that she knew the coyotes were back in the woods. Even though we rarely saw them during the day, Clovis knew they were there. Maybe she didn't want to chance it.

Still, I wished she would come over and sleep near our home. Even my clients would look out the gym windows, looking for her. Sometimes, I would take them outside to do part of their workout so we could also see if Clovis was around. My clients began asking about her regularly. "Have you seen Clovis today? Any updates?" They were always curious to see if I had made any progress. They had to be getting tired of hearing about her. I was like a proud momma talking about her kids. I couldn't stop. These women were beginning to see what the situation entailed.

Because they were at my place three or four times a week, they saw Clovis. They understood her living environment. They sensed my desperation to get her. When on those rare occasions, they would see her limp through the field next to the gym, they would begin to comprehend why my heart was hurting for this little girl. They realized that her living space was being compromised across the street due to the homes going up.

The construction across the street posed other issues as well as diminishing her space. So much debris. So much equipment. Everything seemed to be in the way. And then there was the dirt and mud. Every rain would prove to be a mud bath for Clovis. I would head over to feed her and have to wear mud boots or old yard shoes. I would sink several inches in the mud, trying to reach the spot where I would leave her food. I always smiled as I went over to that lot.

There, in the mud, would be her large footprints. And they were easy to spot since she only ran on three legs. It made me happy to see her prints. Unusually happy. I would come home, telling Randy about her prints, grinning from ear to ear. Why that made me so happy, I'm not quite sure, but it did. Maybe it was because every time I saw a fresh set of her prints, I knew she was still alive. I snapped photos of her pawprints to keep on my phone. All I had to do was look at the photo to make me smile. The day those footprints disappeared would certainly be crushing. I prayed that would never happen! The sun would come out after the rain and dry the prints on the ground. I could have made a cast of her pawprints. They seemed so big! At one point, I think I mentioned it to Randy. I thought it would be nice to have a plaster cast of her prints, much like you do your children's handprints when they are young. I'm sure Randy thought I was crazy, but I never followed through with that craft. The paw prints, however, did prove useful in determining where she would run off to.

My prints were easy to track as well! On more than one occasion, I lost a shoe in the mud. Trying to reach her in that slop was such a mess. It felt like I was walking through quicksand, sinking with every step.

I would lift a foot out of the mud, and the suction sound could be heard echoing across the lot. There would be my shoe, stuck in the mud. On one occasion, while reaching down to try to pull my shoe up out of the mud, I fell. What a sight! I was lying in a mud bath, unable to get myself out. I desperately tried to stand up, but every time I tried, my shoes would either come off or I would sink further into the mud and fall again. Thankfully it was early in the morning, so no neighbors saw this most likely viral video moment. I somehow managed to get myself out of the sinking mud but was covered from head to toe. I hope Clovis realized what it took for me to bring her food! I was also hoping that the owners of the new house didn't mind me being over there, leaving tracks and mud potholes all over their future yard.

It was soon after I lost my shoe in the mud that I met the couple building the new house. Jimmy and Nety Idoski only lived a couple of streets from this new location. I introduced myself and filled them in on the story of Clovis. They, too, had seen her on multiple occasions, as many neighbors had. They were so kind and gracious and seemed to have no problem with me being over on their property. I told them I was trying desperately to get Clovis before their home would be complete, which was estimated to be March-April of 2022. It was now September 2021. Surely, I could get her by then!

Photo Gallery

For more amazing photos and videos, or to see updates to Clovis' story, you can go to our Facebook Page, *I Never Wanted a Dog*. You can also email us at ineverwantedadog@gmail.com.

An early photo of Clovis, caught on our game camera, across the street on the construction lot where she would often hide.

Clovis in our front yard late at night after having eaten her dinner.

A tenacious coyote, creeping up to steal Clovis' food!

One of my favorite early photos of Clovis, resting in our front yard on her blanket.

This is the area on the construction lot we dubbed "the mound."
Clovis would come to spend the majority of her time here in the fall of 2021.

Clovis relaxing on her bed at the mound.

Clovis's hiding spot amidst the construction. She would often sleep behind all the trash among the leaves and debris to hide herself.

Clovis waiting for me to bring her a treat!

Clovis resting near her bed on the construction lot.

Meeting at the "treat board" and finally having success!

Welcome home, Clovis!

Clovis getting love from her new daddy, Randy.

Sweet dreams on her first real bed!

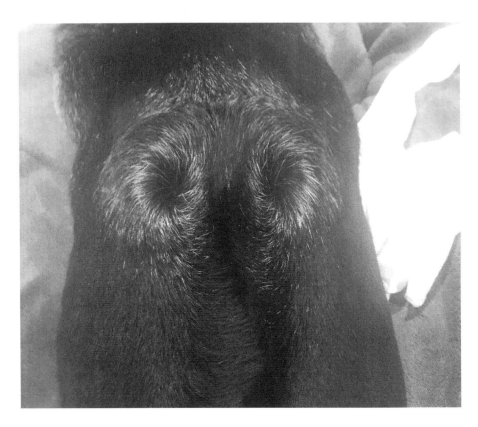

The markings of a Ridgeback dog.

Relaxing in her new backyard, complete with shiny new tags!

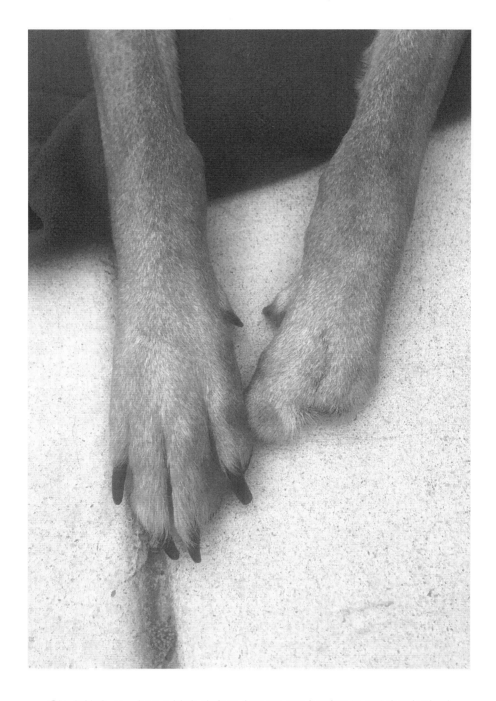

Clovis' left paw has a birth defect, but we are hoping to get that looked at as soon as her heartworm treatment is finished.

Friends and neighbors Tim, Julie, Georgia, and Olivia Lamont.

Friends and neighbors Robby and Paula Ritchey.

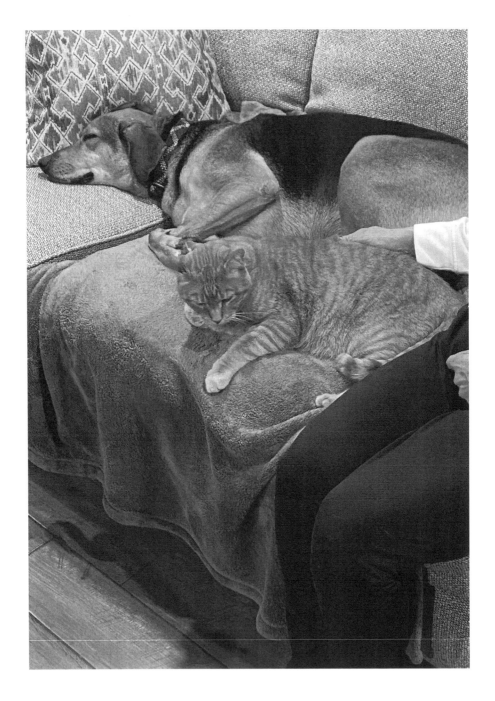

Clovis and new friend, Thomas.

Clovis and new friend, Rocky, who seems perfectly happy
to have Clovis around now.

Clovis is in heaven!

Clovis has never been so loved and so at peace.

Hugs and kisses at last.

Chapter 9

"Therefore, comfort each other and edify one another,
just as you also are doing."

1 Thessalonians 5:11

These fall days were a pleasant break from the summer heat for Clovis. Fortunately, the summer of 2021 didn't see the excessive temperatures that we often encounter for too many days. Some summers, we have several—up to 30 or more—100+ degree days. Not this summer, thank goodness. Still, the heat wasn't pleasant if you were living outside and wearing a fur coat. As September ended and October rolled around, temperatures became much more tolerable. I was less worried about Clovis now, but I knew we might be running out of prime time to win her over. The one thing I kept telling myself was, "We can't let her go through another winter out there!" While our Texas "winters" don't typically hit us until January or February, we sometimes get the occasional ice storm as early as November. I was hoping this winter would be more typical than February 2021. If we could get through the next two to three months with temperatures staying above 40, I would feel more at ease.

Randy was now making multiple trips across the street with me to Robby and Paula's and Tim and Julie's homes to take Clovis treats. As we approached the opening in the chain-link fence, Randy would stop behind the wooden privacy fence and peer through a knothole at Clovis. I would move to the chain-link fence and stand there, talking to her. She would lie in Robby and Paula's one-acre yard, enjoying the warm but not scorching October sun, and stare at me as though she was listening to every word I was saying. After a few minutes, I would set the treat down on the handkerchief near the fence opening, wave to her and bid her goodbye. "Clovis, it's so good to see you! Are you enjoying your nap? I wish you would come to see me! We would take such good care of you! Here's your treat—enjoy it! I'll see you later, OK?" To anyone who might be watching, not knowing the story of Clovis, I'm sure they would wonder why we didn't grab her. Why didn't we just put a leash on her? Why didn't we throw a net or something over her if we were that close? But we knew what we were trying to do, and I felt like it was working. Slowly, but working.

As I walked off, Randy would continue to watch her through the knothole. I can only imagine what it looked like to onlookers. An older man, standing straight up against a wooden privacy fence, face plastered up to a hole, peeking into someone's backyard! Luckily no one ever said anything to us. Robby, of course, knew what we were doing, as did Tim and Julie. Still, it made for a very awkward scene. As I walked away, Randy said Clovis' eyes followed me down the fence line. We would cut back through the front yard to the street, cross to the sidewalk and stand and wait. We could see the opening in the fence where she would come to get her treat. She had learned to wait until she knew we had left the yard. She wanted that treat, but she had patience. She made sure we were far away before coming to snatch it up.

I would call out to her again, and Randy and I would wave and tell her goodbye. I was convinced we couldn't talk to her too much. Was she learning our voices? I know she was.

With multiple trips through the lots and across the street a day for about four to five weeks, we soon realized that Clovis was hanging out at the new construction site more and more. She would be there every morning, waiting for me to bring breakfast. As soon as the construction workers drove up, she would take off back to Robby's yard.

One evening, while out on my front porch with the flashlight, I shined it across the street into the construction lot. Two bright yellow eyes were staring my way. Was this Clovis? Was it a raccoon? I was pretty sure it was Clovis but couldn't tell in the darkness of night. The next morning, I walked over to explore the area. Yes, her large pawprints were all over the place. Why was she back in that corner?

Every morning and every night for a couple of weeks, I would shine my flashlight, and there would be her glaring eyes. I would run and get Randy. "Randy, look! Do you see her eyes?!" I would shine the light to show him the glowing, blinking eyes. There she would be, lying across from our house, staring at us into the night. I was beginning to think she had found that spot so that she could gaze over at my house!

We soon noticed that she started lying on what appeared to be a pile of brush and a few old pallets of grass that were left over from a prior build. This mound was the exact location where I had been seeing her beaming little eyes at night.

It was a mound about 6 feet in length and width and about a foot high. It wasn't perfect, but Clovis loved it there. It was in the far northeast corner of the lot across the street, directly across from our front door. If I went out my front door, I would be looking straight over at her about 75 yards away. Had she chosen this spot so she could watch my house? Surely not. She chose it for a reason though, and I wanted to believe it was because of me.

Randy and I took a bale of straw and a blanket over to the mound. We might as well make it comfier for her! Besides, there was nothing but dirt surrounding the mound—no grass whatsoever in the entire acre of land. When it rained, it was a soggy, muddy, miry pit. Maybe the straw would not only make a nice bed, but if we spread some out, it would cut down on the mud I had to walk through to take her breakfast and dinner every day. This mound was not only in the back corner of the yard, but it was almost right up next to the fence that was behind it. Good choice, Clovis. The fence blocked any north wind coming with the seasons changing. As Randy and I stood back by the mound spreading straw, we could see why she liked the spot. She felt safe. Protected. Hidden. It was far enough away from the construction workers who were on the lot, and there was a row of small trees and brush that she could run behind to escape to the next street over if she had to. Lying on that mound, she could see. She could see all directions. She could see people walking by in the streets with their dogs. She could see coyotes or skunks approaching. And she could see me. Her new bed looked straight at my front porch. The next three months would be a staring contest between Clovis and me.

From that moment on, Clovis seemed to come more and more to her home on the mound. She occasionally went to Tim and Julie's or even into Robby's yard, but the mound was becoming the norm. This was great for me for two reasons: 1) I didn't have to go looking for her everywhere, and 2) it was much easier to take her meals to her. Plus, I could sit and watch her from my porch, which I did. She still napped in other locations on that lot—in the brush, in the corner with all the trash, and sometimes right out in the middle of the lot in the wide open! She would sprawl herself out, looking dead to the world. However, she always knew when someone was approaching and would wake up and run. Maybe it was time to re-evaluate my strategy. I needed to find a way to get closer without scaring her.

On so many occasions, I would head out to go for a walk, and I would see her sleeping in the brush by the side of the road. Her head would pop up as I walked by, and I would call her, "Hi Clovis! I hope you're enjoying your nap!" And I would keep walking. I wanted her to know that I saw her, but I wasn't coming for her. On my return from the walk, I would do the same thing. I might even stop and chat with her from a distance, but again, I didn't want her to think I was going to approach her. I wanted her to get comfortable with me. I wanted her to see that I was friendly but leaving her alone. It was difficult. Everything inside of me wanted to get as close as I could.

I wanted to test the waters and see how far she would let me come. But I also didn't want to go backward in this journey. So, I kept walking. Every day the same thing. Her location might change, but I would find her and walk past her, letting her know I was aware of her but not threatening her. At one point, I even started taking a trash bag with me to pick up trash along the main road in front of the construction sites, close to her napping spot.

I would walk up and down the road where she could see me, picking up trash, talking to her as I went along. She would watch me the entire time, probably wondering if I was going to try to come closer to her. I never did. I stayed on track with my plan and just let her watch me, hopefully feeling more comfortable with my presence. Often, she would look up, listen to me for a minute, and then lay her head back down. Even this was a huge success for me! If she were scared, she would have remained on alert. Wouldn't she have sat up at attention, ready to run? Yes, she most certainly would have. She seemed relaxed, as if she knew I would be her friend. I was convinced that one day we **would** be friends.

While I was thinking those thoughts in my head, Randy was doing what he does best—encouraging me. He told me on multiple occasions, "Stacie, think about it. You are probably the only human who talks to her every day. You are the only person that she has any relationship with. She has been alone for almost three years, and now she has you! You are her whole world right now, even though you may not feel like it. She has no one but you." Randy knew just what to say to me at this point. Others would sometimes tell me similar things. Pat, from across the street, and

Jerry and neighbors down the road—telling me I was Clovis' only real friend. Because they all had dogs of their own, I figured they knew the mind of a dog far better than I did. They understood how Clovis must be feeling. It was enough to motivate me to continue. I thought about what they all said; I knew they were right. Clovis had been completely alone, with no human contact, no physical touch, no one to love on her, for at least three years that we knew of. Now, she had me. Many people had tried to get her. Many people had spoken to her or given her food at one time. But I had been given the time and the opportunity to stick with it every day for several months. I'm sure many other people wanted Clovis to be rescued, but as I mentioned earlier, I had the time during the day that many others didn't have. I couldn't quit. I wasn't going to fail this poor little girl. She needed a home.

Randy knew just what to say to encourage me and make me realize that what I was doing—what I was putting myself through—would be worth it. By this point, I wanted to help Clovis. But she was also helping me. I don't remember another time that I put so much time and effort into something, especially something that had no monetary reward. This was different. Even though I was doing it all for a dog, I felt as though God had commissioned me to this task. Clovis needed me, but I also needed Clovis. I joked that if Clovis ever left and we couldn't find her, I would have to find a new purpose in my life. I had spent so much time in my quest for her that it seemed my entire life revolved around her. I wouldn't know what to do without her! She was my everything. Clovis had become my purpose for this time in my life. With so much going on in the world—the pandemic, the weather, chaos in our government, racial injustices, and people hurting in so many ways, God decided to use this sweet dog to give my life purpose at this point.

At the age of 57, I never dreamed that a dog would be part of God's purpose for me. The Lord has so much He wants to accomplish in us and through us. From spreading the Gospel of Jesus to helping our neighbors and having fulfilling relationships—there are so many things that are part of His purpose in our lives. Yet, He sometimes brings smaller, more seemingly insignificant things into our lives that He uses to teach us and mold us into His likeness. That's what He was doing with me through Clovis. The greater purpose God has for my life brings honor to Him, and I was beginning to see how this was happening.

I would never have dreamed that a dog would lead me closer to God, but He chose to use what I would respond to, what I would relate to.

Pursuing Clovis and longing to bring her peace and happiness was changing my heart in ways I would not have expected. We may never understand why the Lord does things the way He does or when He does them, but I do believe there is always a reason. He was slowly unveiling the many reasons this was happening: patience, faith, trust, love for people, hope for my daughter—what other reasons for this pursuit could He possibly have in store?

Chapter 10

"There is no fear in love; but perfect love casts out fear."

1 John 4:18

Now that Clovis was spending the majority of her time in the lot directly across the street from me, I was able to see her more. Every morning, as usual, I would check the camera set up in my front yard just to see if she had visited in the night. Without a doubt, she would always make her way over after dark. I was still leaving some food but knew that her chances of getting it were slim. I wanted her to know it was there if she needed it. After camera check, it was breakfast time! I began taking Clovis' breakfast to her over by her new home on the mound. As I crossed the street and into the lot, she would pop her head up to see me and trot off to the far west corner on the opposite side of the lot by all the construction trash. But she would wait. I could see her, watching and waiting, peering at me while I set her food down.

I would call to her, "Good morning Clovis! It's time for your breakfast! Come and eat now before other critters come get it!" And I would walk back home. At first, she would wait until I was back on my front porch. But after about two weeks, she was making her way back to the bowl while I was still walking home but not yet across the street.

Even this was progress! I would excitedly tell Randy how she was coming to get her food while I was still close by, beaming at what I thought was such great news. I'm not sure if he was as excited as I was, but as long as I was happy, so was he. He could see my passion for Clovis and knew just how much she meant to me.

I would go back and sit on my porch and just watch her through my binoculars, eating her food and her treat. She was a funny girl. Such a routine. She started snatching up the treat first, running to her straw bed on the mound, and then later eating her bowl of food. It became her ritual.

I would sit and watch as long as I could. Neighbors going to work, school buses coming by to pick up children, and people walking their dogs saw me every morning sitting on my porch, staring through the binoculars. I think the Amazon delivery people even thought I was just waiting out there for a package. Eventually, I would have to go inside to get ready for work. My job was starting to get in the way of my pursuit of Clovis!

About two to three hours after breakfast, I would have a break from my clients. Rushing into the house, grabbing a chicken jerky treat, and switching to my now named "dog feeding shoes," I would walk over to find her. Sometimes she would be on the mound. Other times, she would be lying out in the dirt field. But one thing I did notice: she wasn't leaving when the construction workers came anymore.

This was HUGE! She felt safe enough to stay on that 1-acre lot, even with their trucks and cars pulling in. Even with their music loudly playing. Even with the hammering and nail guns sounding off. She was getting used to us.

As I walked toward her, treat in hand, she would stare at me, knowing I was bringing her something. But still, she would trot off. I would kneel and wave the jerky. I tried sitting in the dirt. I even sat near the trash pile, hoping to ease her feelings of intimidation.

I would sometimes stay for 15-20 minutes, waiting, praying, hoping that she would begin to ease her way over to me.

Talking to her as usual, I would always say the same things: "Clovis, you're such a good girl! I want you to see me and come to my house. I'm not going to hurt you at all. I promise you can trust me! We just want to take care of you. You're such a pretty girl." And she would stare at me, those dark brown eyes piercing it seemed into my soul.

She wouldn't blink or move. It was as if she was scanning me from head to toe, sizing me up to see if I would be good to her. In the last few months, she had gone from running from me if our eyes locked to staring at me as if in a trance. I could have sat there for hours watching her, but it would be time for me to get back to work. I would leave the treat on a handkerchief by the mound. She couldn't wait for me to leave so she could gobble it up! Somehow, even though I was tired and weary of all the time I was spending, I could see glimmers of hope. At least she wasn't running off anymore.

Dinnertime was still in our front yard. When I would see her on her mound in the late afternoon, I would take dinner to her early, hoping she would get to eat it before dark. I couldn't leave it over there after dark, however. As soon as the sun went down, raccoons, opossums, foxes, and coyotes would converge on the bowl of food. I wanted Clovis' sleeping space to be kept secret.

The last thing I wanted to do was draw attention to her and have other animals encroaching on her space to get the food. If she was there before dark, I would take dinner to her. Otherwise, I would set it out in my front yard, hoping she would beat everyone else to it. I knew she was getting breakfast, so at least she had one good meal and several treats a day. That had to be better than the last two years combined.

Clovis was definitely hidden on her home on the mound. We noticed early on that she was very quiet. We never heard a sound from her—not a growl, a bark, even a whimper. And when people or dogs would walk by down the street, sometimes cutting through the lot where she was lying, she would lay as still as she could, statue-like. She wouldn't move. She wouldn't make a sound. It was her way of surviving, we supposed. The quieter she could be, the less likely any person or animal would bother her. If a human or animal approached her, she didn't vocalize or become aggressive. She ran and hid.

She never once showed signs of combative behavior. Her style was to be submissive. Shy. Quiet. Still. This was yet another way she had learned to become invisible. It had worked well for her for three years. We found it interesting that Clovis would lie still and watch owners walk their dogs on leashes down the road right in front of her. What did she think of this? Did she wonder what was happening? Did she know what they were doing, or had she experienced this before? We were surprised that, as a dog, she never felt inclined to run up to another dog to investigate. Most dogs would have barked or acted a bit excited to see another potential friend or foe. Not Clovis. She just remained inconspicuous. Most of the time, no one else noticed that she was there.

Every day, I felt I was getting closer to a breakthrough. I would come home and tell Randy how she wasn't running as far or as fast away from me. How she was coming back to eat the food much sooner after I set it down. How she just didn't seem as scared of all the people working on the house. I wanted to step things up a bit. The only thing I knew to do was more of the same that I had been doing for several months now. Every morning, I would try to get to Clovis before the workers came, mainly so I could sit and talk to her, hoping it would be less stressful with just the two of us.

Thankfully, because of all the delays with supplies due to Covid-19, there were a few weeks when no construction workers came. This was an answer to prayer for me. I needed the time, the quiet, the feeling of safety for Clovis.

I began to take treats and sit as close as possible to her. At times, this meant sitting on the foundation of the new house. The framing was up but not enclosed. I could see her, and she could watch me. I would sit back, relax, and just watch her, letting her know I wasn't coming for her but just enjoying sitting near her. She seemed to be OK with this. As long as I didn't try to approach, she didn't run. I was so excited! I was finally close enough to her to see her more clearly. Tim and Julie were correct—this little girl was part Ridgeback!

Those marks Randy and I had seen on her back over the summer weren't injuries or bloody wounds but hair growing in the opposite direction. We thought Clovis had scraped her back up towards her neck. She had run under so many barbed wire fences that we just knew she had cuts and wounds all over her. But we were wrong! This was the marking of a Ridgeback for sure. I wondered where she could have come from. A beautiful dog, yet out on her own with no one to care for her.

Still unsure of what other mix of breeds Clovis might be, I began looking up information on Ridgeback dogs.

I found interesting facts about the Rhodesian Ridgebacks. Originally from Rhodesia, Africa (now Zimbabwe), the Ridgeback is known as "The African Lion Hound." It was known for its ability to track but never kill lions. Today, they are cherished family dogs but with strong independence. The hallmark of this breed is the ridge on the back, as Julie had pointed out. This is formed by the hair growing in the opposite direction to the rest of the coat. It starts just behind the shoulders and continues down to just before the hips. At the beginning of this ridge are two identical crowns, or swirls, directly opposite each other. Known for their even temperament, the Ridgeback is lovingly devoted and affectionate to his master yet reserved with strangers. They have a quiet, gentle nature and rarely bark. This explained a lot! I read so much more about Ridgeback dogs, but until I could pet Clovis, see her up close, and get to know her better, it would be harder to tell just how much like a Ridgeback she was. For now, though, she showed many signs of that breed: even temperament, quiet, no barking, and most definitely independent.

As I took treats to Clovis, I still couldn't understand what dog wouldn't come running to snatch a treat from my hand. She knew I had it. She knew it was yummy! But she just couldn't bring herself to get it from me. If she was a Ridgeback, she would come to see me as her owner—her person—whom she would trust and be devoted to. Maybe then she would get the treats from my hand. Randy and I began to joke about the treats and the wild animals by our home. As I had mentioned, we have several deer that come into our back field. Three deer, two does and a yearling, come up every morning and night. They visit so often that I had given them names. One doe, Mabel, was a bit more grayish-brown in color, while Ginger, the other, was more reddish-brown. Her fawn, who we later learned was male due to his budding antlers starting to pop through, we named Nutmeg. One afternoon, after discussing why Clovis wouldn't come get a treat from my hand, Randy made a bet with me.

"Stacie, I'll bet you that I can get these deer to come eat from my hand before you can get Clovis to eat from yours."

"You're on!" I said.

I figured he was right. The deer showed more signs of making friends with us than Clovis did. They didn't run when we went out into the yard but stood there, eating the deer corn that Randy would spread. Often, Randy would take a bucket of deer corn out to the field while they were all standing there. They were so familiar with him that he could spread the corn and walk back to the yard, and they would never flinch. Yes, I was beginning to think that Mabel, Ginger, and Nutmeg would make quicker progress than Clovis.

In the next few weeks, Clovis became increasingly more comfortable with me coming to see her by the mound. We seemed to play a game of peek-a-boo at times. I would head over to see her, treat in hand, and as usual, she would get up from her bed and start to head to the west side of the lot near the main road as if she was going to cross the street to Robby's house. She had stopped actually crossing, however. She would find a place to hide near the new home and lie down. This was my cue to go into the framed house and walk through, trying to see just how close I could get to her before she would move again. Clovis was watching, waiting for me to peer around one of the corners at her. Almost on cue, she would get up and trot over to another area by the house and lie down again. I realized she wasn't too scared of me anymore or she would have bolted across the street to the safety of Robby's yard. Yet, there she was, lying in the dirt around another corner of the house, waiting for me to peek at her again.

Sometimes, I would sit inside the house and talk to her. People driving by or those out for a walk could see me inside this framed house, sitting alone. I often wondered what they thought. They had to wonder why I was there and what I was doing—sometimes early in the morning, sometimes in the rain, sometimes in the darkness of night. Some neighbors knew, but what about all the others that passed by this house daily. To look over and see a woman sitting on the slab of a home, seemingly talking to no one, must have been perplexing! Sometimes I would even lie down on the slab, resting and waiting to see if Clovis would approach me. She didn't, but then again, at least she didn't run. I was OK with that for now.

Whenever Clovis would finally close her eyes, I would try to inch my way closer to her. Bit by bit, scooting on my backside closer to her, I almost would be giggling. I would slide over a foot or two and wait. Sometimes she would sense that I was moving and open her eyes. I would talk softly to her, "Clovis, it's OK. I just want to talk to you, sweet girl. Don't worry. I won't come and get you." I wanted to believe she knew what I was saying. Many people said that while she might not understand my words, she understood my tone. That made sense! She could hear in my voice the calm, the kindness, the desire to help her. I believed that she was sensing my love for her. As quickly as she would open her eyes to look at me, she would close them again as if to drift off into sweet dreams. I was beginning to believe it might not be too much longer.

The games of peek-a-boo continued for a few weeks. While I was excited that she wasn't running away, I was tired of the same thing day after day. Some days, I would head over to see her, and there she would be, sleeping on her mound with the blanket we had put out. She would get up to jaunt off a few yards, and I would fix her blanket for her. Every morning, rain or not, the blanket would be covered in dew, making it wet and cold in the fall temperatures. I would shake it and fold it again, allowing the dry side to be up.

I felt as though I was taking care of a child, desperately trying to make her more comfortable. Who knows if she even noticed the dampness of the blanket or that I would dry it for her? But I knew. It made me feel like I was helping her. Placing a treat on the dry blanket, I would walk away and sit somewhere at the construction site and talk to her. She began running back to her treat at the mound, with me sitting about 20 yards away. She still felt safe, and we could watch each other.

A few times, I would head over to her after a rain to find those huge paw prints in the mud. I would track her down and find her waiting on me, knowing I was bringing her food. She very much understood the routine at this point and was always waiting for me every morning.

No longer did I have to go searching the neighborhood for her. I didn't even have to go to Tim and Julie's anymore. This made things so much easier for me. Thank you, Clovis! As I sat down, yes, in the mud but usually on a 2 x 4 from the construction, I would dangle a treat. Still, she wouldn't show any signs of wanting to come to get it. I would talk with her, and she would close her eyes. This was my chance. Sliding myself over the muddy ground, I would inch my way closer. She was allowing this as long as I didn't stand up. Once I discovered this, it was much easier to get closer to her. Muddy and dirty, but easy. Some days I would come home covered in dirt or mud. My family shook their heads, wondering what the crazy woman had been up to. It didn't matter to me. I knew it was working.

Around this time, I had a silly idea, but I was getting more desperate every day. With Clovis lying directly across from my house, she could see everything in my front yard. Along with various wild animals near our home, I have fed birds for several years now. Randy and I have put up several feeders of varying types around the property. I enjoy watching the birds, trying to identify them, and listening to their various calls. With my fascination with the birds, I began making homemade suet for them. My children, all in their 20s or 30s, could see their mother becoming "the crazy bird lady." I had to label the suet that I put in the refrigerator for fear that someone would think it was a peanut butter treat and eat some of it for themselves. Every other day or so, I would walk the yard with a big, five-gallon bucket of wild bird seed, filling all the feeders with seed or suet and the birdbaths with water. I wondered if Clovis was watching me. I'm sure she had no idea that I was feeding birds and taking care of them, but I wanted to believe she did. At least she had the opportunity to see me out in the front yard daily without the concern that I might be coming for her. She could lie there and watch. This was her opportunity to study me for a change.

My next crazy thought involved my cats, Rocky and Thomas. Rocky and Thomas love to go outside, but they are usually in the backyard, which is fenced. Remarkably, neither of my cats can get out of the fenced yard. Rocky, with his surgically repaired hip, along with his large stature, can't jump very well. Thomas can jump, but he is just too scared to venture out. We only allow them out in the backyard during the day, with one of us supervising, as the evenings are just too dangerous with coyotes roaming. The cats do love to hide and play in and around Randy's beautiful landscaping, and every once in awhile, I take them to the front yard for something different.

Rocky and Thomas don't stray, preferring to stay close to home, while I sit in the front yard watching them. I wondered if I took them out in the front yard if Clovis would take notice. Would she see that I was being kind to the cats? Did she even know what cats were? That might sound odd, but I had no idea where she had come from or who and what she had been around in the past. She could see that these furry creatures were similar to her somehow. I hoped she would see me with the cats and have an epiphany: "Look at that woman petting those kitties and playing with them. Maybe she is trustworthy and will be good to me too!" If Clovis only knew how trustworthy we were and how many people around the neighborhood were rooting for her to find a home, she would have bolted across the street to greet me.

Chapter 11

"And just as you want men to do to you,
you also do to them likewise."

Luke 6:31

During the first eight months of actively pursuing Clovis, Randy and I started realizing just how caring and concerned so many neighbors were for Clovis. As mentioned, we had so many donate food to help with our expenses. Others stopping to ask how they might be able to help. One gentleman even offered to build Clovis a dog house for our yard. What hit me the deepest was the number of people volunteering to help with Clovis' future veterinarian bills.

Everyone, including Randy and myself, assumed that she would have health issues. Whether it be ticks, fleas, lesions that were infected, heartworms—the list could go on and on. But that paw. That front left paw was what garnered everyone's sympathies. I wondered if she had something stuck in her paw. I envisioned something like the story of Androcles.

Androcles:
Gratitude is the sign of noble souls

"A slave named Androcles once escaped from his master and fled to the forest. As he was wandering about there, he came upon a Lion lying down, moaning and groaning. At first, he turned to flee, but finding that the Lion did not pursue him, he turned back and went up to him. As he came near, the Lion put out his paw, all swollen and bleeding. Androcles found that a huge thorn was in it and was causing all the pain. He pulled out the thorn and bound up the paw of the Lion, who was soon able to rise and lick the hand of Androcles like a dog. Then the Lion took Androcles to his cave, and every day used to bring him meat from which to live. Shortly afterward, both Androcles and the Lion were captured, and the slave was sentenced to be thrown to the Lion after the latter had been kept without food for several days. The Emperor and all his Court came to see the spectacle, and Androcles was led out into the middle of the arena. Soon the Lion was let loose from his den and rushed bounding and roaring towards his victim. But as soon as he came near to Androcles, he recognized his friend, fawned upon him, and licked his hands like a friendly dog. The Emperor, surprised at this, summoned Androcles to him, who told him the whole story. Whereupon the slave was pardoned and freed, and the Lion let loose to his native forest."

Could it be that simple? If I removed a thorn embedded in her paw, could we become friends? I would have to wait to find out until the day she would let me pet her and examine her paw. In the meantime, friends and strangers alike were offering to help with the cost. Randy and I were overwhelmed with their kindness and compassion.

With everyone seeming to come together for the sake of this stray dog, I once again began to think of how much we were doing to help this poor little animal, yet there were so many people needing help as well. My eyes, it seemed, had been opened further, realizing just how true this was. I always knew people needed help, but it was now glaring at me—hurting people are everywhere. Hurting people are not just in other cities, but they are just around the corner from us. I began seeking ways to help those in need. Everywhere Randy and I would go, my eyes were opened to people who were still struggling to pay rent, buy food, or put gas in their cars. I knew I couldn't help them all. But, I could try to do something for those God brought into my life.

This realization also made me more aware of how blessed Randy and I have been. Good employment, healthy, happy children, a nice home, and loving pets. Yes, we were blessed and needed to bless others as well. We were to bless even those we don't feel like blessing!

Showing kindness and generosity to those we struggle with is not easy. This became even more apparent to me as I would listen to people talk about their pets. On numerous occasions, I heard comments from people about their pets, more specifically, their dogs. I would see posted on Facebook something like, "Forget people. Just let me have my dogs." Or someone would say, "You can have all the people. I only want dogs. They love you unconditionally and are easier to love than people." Another said, "I'm so glad I love animals more than humans." And one more post stated, "The more you meet people, the more you understand why Noah took animals instead of humans." Yes, I knew what they meant—pets are loving, they don't talk back, they don't cause problems, and they don't double-cross you, and on and on. As I began pondering these sayings at this time, my heart began to ache. Yes, our animals are wonderful, and I do love my pets! Sometimes, admittedly, I would rather be with my pets than with some people I know.

With everything I felt God was teaching me, these sayings and thoughts started to haunt me. Why? Why was this bothering me? Then I realized that we are called to love people in the same way we love our animals. That certainly isn't always easy. Pets are easy to love! You honestly don't have to try very hard to love a pet because they love you right back. Luke 6:32-33 states, "But if you love those who love you, what credit is that? Even sinners love those who love them. And if you do good to those who do good to you, what credit is that to you? For even sinners do the same." If we were only called to love those who are nice, those who are kind, those we enjoy being around, that would be one thing. But no. We are called to love all people, even when they don't love us in return. Of course, it's easier to love a pet than some humans! If we are honest with ourselves, I'm sure we would all agree that even we aren't so easy to get along with at times. I started praying that God would help develop this kind of love for other people in me that I had for my cats and Clovis. People are much easier to love when seen through His eyes.

It seemed I was having no trouble loving this seemingly sweet stray dog. What was there not to love? From a distance, she seemed so gentle and submissive. I hoped that if I ever caught her, she would be the kind of dog that would fit into our family. I had to get this baby girl a safe, loving home. Because of this, I continued. So many people cared about Clovis and were hopeful that I would be able eventually to capture her. As November rolled around, she showed signs of giving in to my wooing.

Every day, as I wandered over to the new building across the street where Clovis was now spending the majority of her time, I tried to think of new ways to reach out to her. Most mornings, I left for my run by 5:30 am, first shining my flashlight over to her bed on the mound to see if I could see her eyes glowing in the dark.

Yes, there they were. Two eyes popping up every time I shined the light.

Knowing I had to be back home, food in hand, by 7:00 because that is when the workers started rolling in, I would take off on my run. Even though Clovis wasn't running from the workers anymore, I wanted to feed her and have a few moments to sit and talk to her before they showed up. Pat, the builder, had kept all of them up to date on what was going on. The construction workers knew that I was trying to win this dog over and not to try to approach her or catch her themselves. They were quite cooperative. They would see me sitting out in the dirt, talking with her several times a day.

The mere fact that Clovis allowed this to happen meant that her guard was starting to come down.

I wasn't getting much closer to her, but we were making progress nonetheless. Clovis almost seemed to like having me sit and talk to her. Some of my friends and neighbors would remind me yet again, "Stacie, you're the only friend she has!" And they were right. I think she started looking forward to me coming over for our little visits. In the middle of the lot, in what would be the backyard of the new house, was a pile of wood and debris. One larger board, about six to eight feet in length and about a foot wide, was lying right out in the middle of the dirt. I began to walk over to see Clovis, treat in hand, and sit or lie down on the board. I did it mainly because it gave me a spot to sit, not directly in the dirt and mud. I would visit with her awhile; then, when I felt it was time to leave for work, I would get up, watch her walk off a few yards, and wait. She was waiting for me to take the treat to her blanket on the mound. As soon as I dropped the treat off and bid her goodbye, she would run back, grab it quickly, and find a place to lie down and gobble it up. This went on every day, three or four times a day, for at least three weeks. I'd sit on the board, often lie on the board, hoping this would be less intimidating, and wait to give her the treat.

On occasion, I would head over to the new house and find her sleeping somewhere near the foundation, usually in a shady area.

Even though it was November, it could still be a bit warm for a dog, so she usually found a nice cool place in the dirt to sleep. I decided I would try to get closer to her without her realizing what I was doing. I would walk slowly through the framed house, walls still open to the yard so you could see through very clearly and openly. I found it fascinating, trying to guess what room would be what. Ah, this is the kitchen, and that looks like a large pantry. The living room is right off of the dining area and so on.

As I meandered through the home, I would talk out loud so she could hear me, murmuring to myself about the house. As long as I didn't look directly at her, she was fine with me getting closer. The minute I turned to stare, she would get up and move. However, she would only move to another spot, lie down again, and watch me. Clovis was used to looking directly at me by now, but she wasn't quite ready to let me in her personal space. I continued with this every day for about a week or two, making sure not to get so close as to make her uncomfortable. Walking through the house, sometimes sitting down in one of the rooms, I would talk to her. Finally, one day, I turned around to face her, to find that she had come closer to me while I had my back turned to her. She had been lying outside the foundation of the house while my back was turned to her. As I walked through the house, talking about whatever came to my mind, she got up and came inside the house to be closer to me! I wasn't sure what to do, so I just sat down right where I was, and we stared at each other. I talked, and she listened. We must have been there for half an hour, and she listened to every word I was saying.

Not wanting to cause her more anxiety or fear, I finally said, OK, Clovis. This has been so fun talking to you, but I'm going to leave you alone now. I need to go home, but I promise I'll be back later, OK?" I slowly got up and walked home, everything in me not wanting to leave her alone. I felt like I could have stayed all afternoon, but I wanted her to know I wasn't trying to capture her. I was just there to visit, and I would visit again very soon.

Thanksgiving weekend was coming up and in the back of my mind, so was possible winter weather. While we don't usually have horrible, cold, snowy days in November, we have an occasional ice storm. The kind that blankets trees with so much ice that limbs fall and break. Power lines come crashing down, and driving is next to impossible. I didn't see anything like this in the forecast. Still, I wondered how much longer I had before I would have to begin preparing myself for the inevitable cold weather and how I would handle seeing Clovis possibly have to live through it again.

I would come home to Randy, crying, "Randy, what am I going to do? I can't watch her go through that again this year! I can't!" And Randy, sweet as always, would reaffirm what I was doing, but he later told me that deep down, he was worried too. He was worried for me as well as Clovis. He knew how much I was hurting for her, and he didn't want to see me in so much agony.

Thanksgiving week proved to be a week for which to be truly thankful. I had taken off from work from noon on Wednesday through the weekend.

Four and a half days of no work whatsoever. We had Thanksgiving dinner at our house, but just with our immediate family. Felice was in Alabama working and unable to come home, so it was just the five of us—Randy, myself, Natalie, Sydney, and Mylon. I could handle that. It would be nice to cook a good Thanksgiving meal, but with no guests this year, I didn't worry much about the house or the other usual things you take into consideration when entertaining. What this really was saying to me was "You have more time with Clovis!"

I had four full days to try to win her over, and I took advantage of every minute. Mornings were cool, but I love cold weather for running. It's exhilarating, and I look forward to fall and winter mornings. This was no exception. I left the house every morning for my run, shined my light to see her eyes appear, and waved to Clovis, telling her I would be back soon with her food. Then I would rush over to the lot to feed her and talk to her upon my return. Because we were having our Thanksgiving dinner on Friday, I had Thanksgiving Day to spend with my new love, Clovis. Bright and early, after my run and with the sun just starting to come up, I headed over to the lot to find my sweet girl and take her a treat along with breakfast. As I crossed my street and approached the lot, I saw her—running around in circles, acting playful and excited! She would crouch down, tail up in the air, and then jump up and run around again. This was a first! Usually, she would wait for me calmly and quietly. Today, she was acting more like a real dog. A dog that was excited to see her owner coming with a treat! My heart was so joyful that I almost started crying. As I approached her, treat in hand, telling her my usual "good mornings," she was so excited, tail wagging, jumping around with the energy of a puppy. Then she did something I had never seen or heard before. She barked! Just one excited bark, but it was enough. She was genuinely happy to see me!! This was the biggest breakthrough yet. I had never heard a peep out of her, let alone a full-fledged bark. All those months and years of being out on her own, avoiding people and other animals, she had never let out a growl or a whimper. And now here I was, the proud recipient of what seemed to be her first bark. She was talking to me! I went to the large board where I had started sitting, and she ran excitedly closer to me but still left a good distance between us, maybe 15 feet.

She sat down and just stared at me. I waved the treat, holding it out so she might want to get it from me, but she wasn't ready. She just sat still, staring. What discipline she had to keep from running over to grab the treat! After talking with her for a few minutes, I stood up, left the treat on the board, and started walking over to the mound where I would place her food bowl.   I stopped to turn and look, and there she was, grabbing the treat and running off to enjoy it. She didn't go far. I could still see her a few yards away near a large pile of construction debris. She would be over to get her breakfast soon.

As I walked home, smiling from ear to ear, I couldn't wait to tell Randy about Clovis talking to me!   When I reached my front porch, I saw her eating her breakfast.

I gave her an hour or maybe two before going back to see her again. While I wanted to spend time with her, I also didn't want to be a nuisance or a bother. The last thing I wanted was for her to think, "Oh great, here comes that lady again, bothering me while I'm trying to nap." I gave her some time. But I couldn't wait to get back over there. I told Randy about her bark and how excited she was, running around in circles like a real dog does when playing. I'm not sure he understood the significance for me, but I think he was beginning to. Because he didn't see what she did, I think he had a hard time envisioning what I was describing.

After my shower and breakfast, I walked over to find her about mid-morning, not seeing her on the mound where she would usually be. Maybe she went to Tim and Julie's for a change? I took the treat and began walking through the lot, cutting through to the next street over, where I would then cross to their house. But before I even got off the lot, I almost stepped right on Clovis! She was knocked out solid, sleeping in the brush near the spot I would cut through. I barely saw her in time.   Not wanting to surprise her or startle her, I quickly backed up, as quietly as I could, and sat down on the edge of the foundation of the house, about 10 yards away. Then, I waited. I didn't say a thing, knowing that she would eventually smell me. I was right. Within about two minutes, her head popped up. She looked right at me and just lay there, staring. She didn't get up. She didn't leave. And then?

She put her head back down! Eyes still wide open, but chin resting on her paws, watching me.

I had tried so many things to draw this girl closer to me, and while it seemed to be slowly working, I was suddenly overcome by frustration and sadness. I began to cry. Very softly at first—just teary eyes to begin with. I began asking God, "Why is this taking so long? I have been trying everything I can think of, everything I know to do, but she still won't come to me." As the tears began to flow more readily, I noticed something:

Clovis popped up her head, ears coming to attention, head tilting to the side. She was looking at me as though she wondered why I was crying. She had a look on her face of concern! I was fascinated by this—she knew that something was wrong. I began to talk to her, telling her everything was OK but that I just wanted her to come to me so I could take care of her. We sat there at the house for over an hour, watching, talking, listening.

Clovis had finally closed her eyes, listening to me talk to her. I decided to now be quiet and give her a chance to nap while I sat quietly and watched.

She appeared to be sleeping, or at least relaxing, eyes closed. She had to be getting used to me. This same girl that was lying not 10 yards away from me with her eyes closed was the same girl who would frantically run from me or anyone else if we dared to look at her from half an acre away just a few months ago. I slid closer to her. Still sitting on the edge of the foundation, I slid down the edge about 6 inches at a time.

I would slide over and wait, making sure I didn't disrupt her nap or make her uncomfortable. Her eyes opened, she looked at me, then drifted back to apparent sleep. I slid again, another six inches closer. Her eyes would open, but I guess I was still far enough away that she didn't feel the need to move. This continued for another 20 minutes until I was about 10 feet away.

Clovis opened her eyes. I must have been too close as she got up to leave. But then, rather than running off, she backed up about 5 feet and laid back down! She wasn't scared enough to run, but she needed more of a buffer between us. I sat on the corner of the foundation for another hour before telling her, "Clovis, I need to go home now and get some things done. I wish you would come with me! I'm going to leave so you can get a good nap, and I'll be back in a little bit. I love you, sweet girl!" And as I stood up to leave, she lay there watching me. She didn't seem frightened. She didn't seem worried. It was as though she finally realized that I wasn't going to come and grab her. I couldn't wait to tell Randy!

Chapter 12

"And the peace of God, which surpasses all understanding, will guard your hearts and minds through Christ Jesus."

Philippians 4:7

The rest of Thanksgiving Day was a happy one for me. I kept thinking of how Clovis showed such excitement to see me and get her treat. She truly looked happy for a change.

She had always been fairly quiet and calm. But not that morning—it was as if she was a new dog. Running around in circles, front paws down and rear end up, tail wagging, asking me to play with her. This was a change of countenance! "Wait till I tell Robby and Paula or Tim and Julie! They won't believe it till they see it," I thought. No one had ever seen Clovis do anything other than run. Now she was reacting to me out of curiosity and frivolity and not out of fear. I would have to tell them what was happening after the Thanksgiving holiday. For now, I had more work to do. Of course, I would go over again that day to see her as usual. I was beginning to spend three to four hours a day with Clovis. This time off from work was just what I needed.

Later in the afternoon that same day, I went back to see her again. She was not as enthusiastic as earlier in the day, but we went through the same ritual as always—me bringing her a treat and her just staring at me. I sat on the board, treat in hand, trying to coax her over to me. She did manage to come closer, sitting about 10 feet away from me but still not budging toward me. As I sat there, thinking, I wondered about something. If my tears had caused her to notice me or spark an interest in what I was doing or feeling, maybe something else would.

Singing. I decided I would try singing to her. I had been talking to her all this time and praying for her out loud so she could hear me. What if I sang? I saw how she responded to my crying. The more I thought about it, the more it made sense. Animals love music too. I knew that from my cats. I sometimes play the piano, and whenever I sit down to play, Rocky comes running! He will sit next to me, listening intently, purring the whole time. My children are all musicians, and anytime one of them begins to play their instrument, the cats come to listen.

Sydney will be in her room, playing her keyboard or her guitar, and Rocky wants to be in her room so he can listen. Mylon is a trumpet player, and on those occasions, when he pulls out his horn and begins to play, all ears go up, and Rocky will migrate towards Mylon's room.

Even Felice's cat, Mr. Biscuit, loves listening to her when she plays the piano, sitting in the nearby window while she plays. What did I have to lose by trying?

I sat there on the board, trying to decide what to sing. And at that moment, I could think of NOTHING! In all my years of listening to music, all my years of singing at church, all my years of playing the piano, I couldn't think of one single song. My mind had gone blank for some reason. I tried to think of songs from church, thinking those would be a great place to start. We sing praise and worship songs every Sunday. I listen and sing along all the time at home and in the car. Why can't I think of anything? I would think of a song from church, only to realize that I didn't have it memorized. I was so used to reading the words from the screen at church that I hadn't memorized entire songs, only parts. So, I tried thinking of songs I grew up with—classic rock songs from the 70s. Still nothing. Where were the Aerosmith and Queen songs I thought I knew so well? Surely, I could at least remember a John Denver song? What was wrong with my mind? Finally, after about five minutes of searching every corner of my brain, I thought of a song.

Incredible. The only song I could think of was "Jesus Loves the Little Children." I laughed out loud. How could it be that this is all I could pull out of my head? Nevertheless, I began to sing.

Jesus loves the little children,
All the children of the world.
Red and yellow, black and white,
They are precious in His sight.
Jesus loves the little children of the world.

As crazy as it sounds, it did something. Clovis looked up, her ears popping up from their usually floppy position, and listened. When I saw her inquisitive response, I changed the words to add her to the song.

Jesus loves the little doggies.
All the doggies of the world.
Red and yellow, black and white,
They are precious in His sight.
Jesus loves the little doggies of the world.

If people heard me, they would have laughed, but it was no laughing matter to me. Clovis was responding!

I even changed it, yet again:

Jesus loves my little Clovis,
All the doggies of the world …

I wondered if the reason I couldn't think of any other song that day was because this was the song that God wanted me to sing to her. Is that crazy? Maybe. I was beyond caring about being crazy. I must have sung that song a dozen times before another one from childhood popped into my mind.

Jesus loves me this I know,
For the Bible tells me so.
Little ones to him belong,
They are weak, but He is strong.
Yes, Jesus loves me!
Yes, Jesus loves me.
Yes, Jesus loves me.
The Bible tells me so.

Again, Clovis reacted to my singing as if listening intently to every word. I felt like I had found another means of reaching her.

Of course, I had to put her name in there as well. "Jesus loves you, this I know, for the Bible tells me so. Little Clovis to Him belongs, she is weak, but He is strong …." I would sing these two songs, and later a few others that I remembered, to her whenever I would sit with her. I wish I knew what she thought of the singing.

I didn't care if she liked my voice, but was the singing soothing to her? Did she find rest while listening? Sometimes when I would sing, she would lay her head down and close her eyes, almost as if she were enjoying the serenading. By now, I pondered whether I could get close enough to throw a net or something over her to catch her finally. But every time I considered it, I knew it wasn't the right thing to do. I would terrify her and lose the nine months I had spent gaining her trust. I would have to continue to be patient and let her close the gap with me. Not the other way around.

Friday morning, the day after Thanksgiving, I did my usual flashlight eye check, followed by my run and then my Clovis routine. Again, she was excited and playful, prancing around the open lot. No barking this day, but that was OK. I knew every day couldn't be miraculous, but I would take what I could get. I spent two hours with her that morning, singing, talking, and wooing her, before having to head home to begin cooking for our Thanksgiving feast. I would have loved her to be there with us, sitting at our feet in the dining room. Maybe next year? I spent the rest of the morning cooking and preparing for the meal, which we had planned on having around 2:00 pm. It was a wonderful time together, filling the kids in on what was happening with Clovis but not knowing if they understood just what all I had been doing for her. I imagine they were getting tired of hearing about it all the time, but they never said anything about it. They would occasionally walk over to the lot with me to check on her, but otherwise, it was just me, going alone. Randy would go with me across the street about once a day to see her, which I appreciated. Besides, I told him he probably needed to come with me more for Clovis to get used to him. It wouldn't do much good for her to feel comfortable with me if she was still going to run from everyone else in our family.

Thanksgiving at our home always calls for a roasted turkey, as many people have for their family feasts. Cleaning up after dinner is what I hate most. And the worst? Carving up the rest of the turkey, deboning it, and cleaning it all up. I was a bit excited this year as I knew I had a turkey neck waiting for Clovis! I knew that bones weren't recommended to give to dogs, but this was such a delicacy. Yet again, Google helped me out. I looked up information on giving bones to dogs and was pleasantly surprised to find that the turkey neck is fine for them. It's a softer bone in segments—not long splintery bones like a drumstick. I set aside the neck for her with all the bits and pieces of meat that I cleaned off the bones I knew we wouldn't use. I had an entire baggie full of turkey meat and one large neck bone. I could hardly wait to take it to her!

That afternoon, when we had finished our meal and time together, I decided it was time to see her and take the Thanksgiving treat to her. As I approached, she could smell that turkey. Wow, could she smell it! She popped up and came running towards me, but then, in disappointment, she stopped about 15-20 feet away. At first, I thought she was going to come straight to me! How that little girl had such discipline, I will never understand.

But she did. She sat there, looking at me as if to say, "I see what you have there, lady. Just give it to me already!" I went to the board, which had become our official "greet and treat" center, and placed the neck bone down on the board. As soon as I stood up and began to walk back, she snatched it up and ran with it to her safe spot on the mound. She devoured that neck bone and had a good Thanksgiving along with the rest of us.

Later in the evening, when I took Clovis her dinner before it was dark, I added some of the turkey bits and juice to her dry food.

She was in for a treat for the next few days, as long as I had leftovers. Saturday and Sunday of Thanksgiving week were just as thrilling and successful as the first two days. Because of the holiday, no construction workers came for the entire four days I had off from work. It was perfect! I had so much time to spend with her that I was falling behind in things I needed to do at home. I was beginning to feel a bit guilty for not keeping up with dishes, laundry, and cleaning, as well as practically abandoning my husband. Randy never said a word about my absence. He knew how important this was to me. He knew how my heart ached for her. Plus, I think he realized I was getting close. I was hoping that maybe I would have Clovis within the next two months, but Randy still thought it was a long way off. He reminded me that if the building timeline for the house was on schedule, a fence would be going up soon. They were nowhere ready for that, as construction had slowed tremendously due to supply problems with building materials. The Covid-19 pandemic was still being felt in many ways, one of which was the slow supply chain. So many items were either unavailable or back-ordered for months. I felt badly for Jimmy and Nety, the owners, but deep down, I was relieved that I would have more time. Randy was afraid winter was coming, and Clovis would still be there. I think he was more worried about me and my emotions than for her.

As my Thanksgiving break was ending, I was thrilled at what had happened but discouraged that I would now have to go back to work. I couldn't wait to tell my clients about it! They had become accustomed to hearing me talk about Clovis, and now I had something exciting to tell them. They were all such good sports about it. Supportive in every way they could be. They may have been rolling their eyes, thinking, "Seriously, you're talking about this dog again?" But they never let on that they felt that way. My clients are some of the best in the world and always acted as though they were excited to hear how everything was going. I would probably have to treat them to a celebration dinner if I ever did get this little girl to our home.

On my final day of the break, I realized it would be the last day I had for a while to spend a lot of time with her. I grabbed an extra blanket I had put away for such occasions, grabbed a book to read, my phone, and a treat. I headed over to the lot, scanning the dirt field, trying to decide where to put the blanket. This time the blanket wasn't really for Clovis. It was for me. I spread it out right in the middle of the lot, sat down, and called to her.

"Clovis! I brought you another treat. Why don't you come over here and sit on the blanket with me?"

Nothing. She just stared. I went to our usual "treat area" on the board. She had become quite accustomed to meeting me in that particular spot. She now recognized it as the rendezvous board. I left the treat on the board and headed back to my blanket. She immediately scurried over to grab it, headed back to her bed on the mound, and enjoyed the kabob. I lay there on the blanket, reading, looking at my phone, just spending time there. I was hoping she might get curious about what I was doing and why I was there. I sang to her but just stayed right on the blanket. After 20-30 minutes, I had another idea—one that I thought was brilliant. I remembered how she reacted the day she saw me crying. Could that do the trick? I almost felt guilty for trying it, but what did I have to lose? I laid on the blanket on my side, covered my face with my hands, and began to fake cry. "Clovis, (sniffle, sniffle sob) come help me (sob a little more)!" I peeked out from my hands, and she came RUNNING to the blanket! Stopping just shy of the edge of the blanket, she stood, staring at me as if to ask, "What's wrong, Mama? Are you OK?"

I was flabbergasted! It had worked! She failed to come up onto the blanket itself, but she had responded to my cry, my need. Clovis cared about me! I sat up to look at her, and she laid down just a few feet away. We talked for a few more minutes before I found myself too excited not to run home and tell Randy the amazing news.

I ran into the house, "Randy, Randy, guess what!?" I recounted the story to him, about to burst with joy. I'm not sure he believed she came to me at first, but he could see how excited I was. He was relieved to know that Clovis was beginning to respond. Randy was getting tired from all of this, too, I'm sure. The rest of the day, I continued to sit on my blanket and talk with her, though I didn't pretend to be hurt or sad again. While I did feel guilty about tricking her, at least I knew she cared. She had shown me compassion in return. I was finally becoming her "person."

Monday morning after Thanksgiving, November 29th, I was again sitting with Clovis on the board across the street, singing to her.

I had left the blanket at home as I didn't have the time to stay with her as I had the previous days. This time, another old-time church song popped into my head:

"Peace, peace, wonderful peace coming down from the Father above. Sweep over my spirit forever, I pray, in fathomless billows of love."

This song, in particular, I found perfect for singing to Clovis. I had always worried about her stress and anxiety level. She had lived in fear for almost three years, and I wanted her to be at peace. Peace when being with me but also peace while sleeping. I wanted her to feel the peace of God that surpasses all understanding. She needed that. So, I kept singing that chorus, inserting her name, "Peace, peace, wonderful peace, coming down from the Father above. Sweep over dear Clovis forever, I pray, in fathomless billows of love."

This became our anthem. I continued to sing other songs, but this particular one had deeper meaning to me and for Clovis. I wanted peace for Clovis more than anything else. I believed God would give her that peace so that she would not only rest for a change but so that she would trust me more every day. When I sang it to her, she would close her eyes, lay her head down, and rest. It was beautiful to see.

Chapter 13

"Be still and know that I am God; I will be exalted among the nations, I will be exalted in the earth!"

Psalm 46:10

Thursday, December 2nd, started like a normal day and routine. I had run, fixed her food bowl, and sat on the large board, coaxing her with a treat. Today, after ten long months, Clovis decided it was time to approach me for the treat.

As I sat on the board, holding the treat out as far as I could from my body, she came running towards me but put on the brakes before reaching me. She stopped about six feet away, tilting her head and looking at me as if to say, "Toss it to me!" I held it out for her to come closer and take it from my hand. She was holding out for me to gently toss it her way. We were at a standstill. I waited a bit longer, singing to her and waving the treat, but she decided to lie down. We were so close! I could see her little injured paw stretched out in front of her and only a few feet from me. It didn't look torn up, bloody, or even cut. What could be wrong? I noticed that it looked like it wasn't all there—like it was smaller than the right front paw. Had it been cut off in a trap of sorts? It didn't look like it had. If so, it had been such a long time ago that it had healed from the wounds. That's all I could see, but it was more than I knew before.

After 15 minutes of this standoff, I decided to toss the treat to her. After all, she had come this far. From avoiding humans at all costs to coming TO me and laying within a few feet was miraculous. I held the treat out, then gently tossed it about a foot away from my hand. Clovis jumped up, grabbed it, and ran about ten yards back to enjoy it. I counted it a success! She had come to ME. She had pretty much asked ME for the treat! She was finally closing the gap between us. I wondered how much longer it would be before she would take it from my hand.

Later that day, the same routine. Friday, even more of the same-always coming for the treat but staying just shy enough away to not take it from me. I could drop it right under my hand, and she would come snatch it up. But take it from my hand? No way. By Saturday, December 4th, I was perplexed, confused. I sat there with this homeless dog, who I had been wooing for ten months now, and I couldn't figure it out. Why won't she get it from my hand? I began inquiring of God. "Lord, she knows she can trust me. She knows I am the one bringing her food and water. She knows I provide her treats, bed, and everything she needs. Why does she come only when she wants something? Why won't she just come to me and sit with me?" And almost immediately, the thought that went through my mind, which I knew was God, said, "Don't you do the same to Me?" Dagger in my heart! Yes, He provides for me. He gives me all I need. And yet, I wait until I want or need something to come to Him. Like I wanted Clovis to sit next to me, the Lord said, "Stacie, I want you to sit with me too—not just when you need something." I had heard this many times in church or Bible study. To hear it directly from God Himself pierced my heart. I began to cry, telling Him how sorry I was for acting like Clovis, only trusting Him when I needed or wanted something. The story of Mary and Martha came to my mind in Luke 10:38-42:

> *"Now it happened as they went that He entered a certain village; and*
> *a certain woman named Martha welcomed Him into her house.*
> *And she had a sister called Mary, who also sat at Jesus' feet and heard*
> *His word. But Martha was distracted with much serving, and she*
> *approached Him and said, 'Lord, do You not care that my sister*
> *has left me to serve alone? Therefore, tell her to help me.' And Jesus*
> *answered and said to her, 'Martha, Martha, you are worried and*
> *troubled about many things. But one thing is needed, and Mary has*
> *chosen that good part, which will not be taken away from her.'"*

It's not that what Martha was doing was bad. She was serving! Jesus was saying she needed to sit at His feet, like Mary, and be with Him. That was the "good part" He was talking about. I needed to sit with Him.

Ten months after beginning this endeavor, God taught me things every day. He knew what it took to reach me. Clovis had become a way for Him to teach me the things He wanted me to learn. I only hoped that He was almost done teaching me so that I could go ahead and bring Clovis home!

I found myself apologizing to Clovis, feeling like I needed to let her know it was OK to be timid. It was OK to be unsure of me. I told her I knew she must have had a rough life, and it was hard for her to learn to trust me. "Clovis, I promise you, we will always take good care of you! You won't have to worry about hiding, running from coyotes, or scavenging for food. We want to give you a great life!" When I heard myself say that, I knew I could never give her up to anyone else.

I had realized that a few months ago, but now it was real. I was getting so close to having her, and the thought of giving her to anyone was incomprehensible. She was meant to be in our family. She was needed in our family as much as we were needed by her. I couldn't wait for the next weeks to unfold.

Sunday, the 5th, started as usual. I was on my way to greet Clovis and take her breakfast when she saw me crossing the street. She jumped up from her bed and came running towards me with excitement and happiness, tail wagging, looking right at me! But she stopped short of coming all the way. She had been anxiously waiting for me, lying on her bed, staring at my house, longing for me to come. The minute I stepped out my front door and towards the road in front of my house, she hopped up and ran towards me. I was so happy I could barely stand it! I walked further back to where I always put her meal, and as I did, she ran off to the side a bit, still watching every move I made.

I spoke my usual pleasantries with her and turned to go home. She didn't even wait till I was gone---I had no more than turned around and taken three steps, and she was there at her bowl. I just sat down in the dirt and watched her. She didn't seem to mind at all. When she finished, she lied down and stared right back at me. I stayed with her for half an hour or so, just doing my usual visiting and singing before deciding to go home and try to get some much-needed work done around the house.

After a couple of hours of housework, what else was there to do but go back to see Clovis? I went to the kitchen, grabbed a treat, and went back over, hoping she would come closer and take the treat from my hand. As I approached, once again, she came running. She was so happy to see me! It was as if this poor homeless, friendless doggie finally realized she had a friend—a true friend. I knelt on one knee and held the treat out. To my surprise, she came incredibly close, sniffed the treat in my hand, and then gave my hand a little lick! I thought to myself, "I can't believe this is happening!" I think it surprised her because she then jumped back a foot or two. I laid the treat down directly under my hand so she would at least have to come closer to me.

I didn't want to toss it to her this time, now that I knew she wasn't as scared and might come to me. Still kneeling, I dropped the treat, and she snatched it up and ran to her hiding spot behind a rock pile to eat it in peace. I took this as a sign to give her a break and leave for a bit.

It was so hard for me to go back home this time. She had been so close! I could have reached out and touched her or grabbed her, but then what? Would that have terrified her? Probably so, so I decided to hold back. Besides, it now seemed that every day something new was happening. If I continued to be patient, I knew she would continue to trust me more and more. The rest of that afternoon, all I could think of was how that lick felt on my hand. Such a small gesture, but it was so sweet, as if she was telling me she knew who I was, and she approved. I wondered what the next step would be.

After almost a year of creeping along at a snail's pace, things were now starting to go full throttle. Later that Sunday, I headed over, this time in my grungy sweat pants and dog shoes, along with a big towel to sit on so I wouldn't have to keep getting dirty. Too bad I didn't think of this before. I knelt on one knee, this time on the towel near the board, and waited for her arrival. She knew by now what this all meant. She knew it was treat time! I spoke to her quietly and said, "Hi Clovis, it's me again. I brought you another treat because you have been such a good girl! Why don't you come over here and get it? I won't hurt you. I want you to have your treat!" She came jaunting over, cautiously approached me, and looked straight into my eyes. She had the most beautiful dark brown eyes I had ever seen. And she looked so clean and healthy! I couldn't believe that this dog was a stray just by looking at her physical condition.

She was on the thin side, but that was to be expected. Still, she didn't look like she was starving. She was starting to look like she was filling out a bit. I'm sure all the meals and treats were finally catching up with her.

I wasn't worried about her having too much food; she was probably incapable of overeating.   As I held the treat out, I wondered if she would do her usual trick of backing up and begging me to toss it to her. I waited patiently, holding the kabob out for her, and slowly she approached. Finally, she grabbed it from my hand! In her excitement, she grabbed it so quickly that she bit my hand, not meaning to. It didn't hurt or break the skin, but I could tell this was new to her. I screeched, not from pain but from being surprised. I think she realized that she had bitten me due to the quizzical look on her face. She ran off and gobbled it up, and I knew right then that this was the biggest breakthrough yet! Wait till Randy hears about this!

I ran home to tell him what had happened and encouraged him to come with me the next trip over. He was afraid he might scare her, but she had seen him enough on his earlier trips with me to Tim and Julie's that I felt confident she would recognize him. We waited a couple of hours and headed back with a chicken jerky treat this time. As we approached, Clovis came running. When she saw Randy, she put on the brakes but didn't run away. She sat down and just watched us. I started making my way toward her, and Randy stood behind me a few steps. I told him she needed to get used to his smell, and even with him standing a few feet away, she would get to know him.   He knelt on one knee and held out the jerky, but she wasn't ready to come to him yet.

After waiting for a few minutes, I got the treat from Randy and walked toward her. Sitting down on my towel, I held the jerky out, and she slowly came over and snatched it from my hand again. This time, ever so gently. It was as though she had figured it out. She knew she had bitten my hand the last time, and she very delicately lifted it out of my palm this time. Randy was now a true believer! We headed home for the evening after delivering her official dinner and prayed she would be safe for yet another night. This had become my nightly prayer for Clovis. She had been kept safe all these months, and I wanted to know she would be safe for another night, out there in the dark, with no one.

Randy and I went home, had our dinner, finished up whatever work we had to do around the house, and went to bed. Because the temperatures this particular week were unusually pleasant for December, we had our bedroom window open a bit to get some cool fresh air while we slept. Our bedroom is on the front of the house, with our double window over the bed to the east. Around 3:00 am, I awoke from a dream where I heard barking! Was that in my dream? Was it a real dog barking? I had only heard Clovis bark once, but I knew what I heard.

It was Clovis! I jumped out of bed and ran straight to the north-facing window. I pulled up the blinds, and there she was: directly across the street in the neighbor's driveway, face to face with a coyote! I ran to the front door, flipped on the porch light, and opened the door. I yelled to her, and she immediately looked over at me.

The coyote ran off, back behind our house and into the woods, and Clovis ran the opposite direction. I hurried back to tell Randy, but there was nothing more we could do at that moment, other than pray, go back to bed, and hope she would be OK for the remainder of the night.

Monday morning, December 6th, I went to see her for our usual breakfast around 7:00 am. It just made me happy seeing her tail swinging back and forth wildly instead of tucked between her hind legs.

She was giddy, and so was I! I delivered her meal right on time and brought the old bath towel with me to sit on. I spread the towel out not far from her bed and sat to watch her eat. She didn't seem to mind me watching anymore.

No more binoculars and looking out from my porch. I could sit a few yards away and talk to her while she ate. I told her how happy I was that she scared the coyote away and that she was safe. I wanted to believe that she somehow knew what I was saying. While it had taken me all these long months to get this far, it also seemed like it was just yesterday that I had first seen her out my front window, running from the world of humans and into the woods.

I was running a bit late for work, so I scurried off to go home and change my clothes and into my regular shoes, leaving my muddy dog shoes on the porch like always. I headed to the gym to greet my first client of the day, and she could see that I was beaming from the weekend's events. I had to fill her in on how Clovis licked my hand and how she was now anxiously greeting me every morning. I had about three hours of work before my next break, and they were becoming some of the longest hours of my life. Around 10:30, I had a break, so I dashed inside to grab a treat, changed back into my dog shoes, and left for the lot.

I grabbed the towel on my way out the front door and went directly to the construction site. As she saw me coming, I spread the towel out on the ground and knelt on one knee again. She came closer, left paw drawn up off the ground as usual, and reached her nose towards my hand to get the treat. As she took it from my hand, again with the gentleness of a lamb, I slipped my hand under her chin so I could lightly brush my fingers against her.

She froze. I kept contact with her chin and very slowly guided my hand up to the top of her head, and petted her so very gently. Clovis stood like a statue. Her eyes were the only thing moving to and fro. She was looking from side to side as if to say, "What's happening? What's going on? What is this feeling I'm having?" After only about ten seconds, she jumped back a couple of feet.

As quickly as she jumped back, she came right back to me, this time nose pointing down, tucking her head underneath my hand and nudging it as if to say, "Please do that again!" And so, I did. This time she let me pet her for a few more seconds, letting me run my hand down the back of her neck and to the spot where we thought she had wounds from the barbed wire. No wounds—just swirls of fur, indicative of a Ridgeback dog! I was relieved! Once again, she jumped back, telling me with her body, "That's enough for now." I had tears welling up in my eyes. I had waited ten months for this, and I know Clovis had waited at least three years. The reality that this might have been her first touch, her first expression of human love, thrilled me. I wanted to pet her more and hold her, but that was more than she could handle right then. Besides, I had to once again get back to the gym. What struck me afterward was that I never even thought about what might happen if she didn't want me to touch her. What if she had bitten me? What if she attacked? What about diseases, fleas, or other parasites? I never had a single serious thought of any of those things. Clovis and I were buds. I could never in a million years envision her hurting me, and from what I could tell, she looked very healthy for a stray of three years.

I ran home as I had one last set of clients coming in at noon. I work with three ladies at a time during that hour, and they have had their fill of my Clovis stories. But today, even they would be in for a surprise. As they came in the door, one by one, I couldn't help but shout out, "Clovis just took a treat from my hand! She let me pet her!!!" We had a little cheering party as I told them all about it. I jokingly said to them, "Let's hurry and do this session so I can get back to the important stuff of loving on Clovis!" They were so happy for me and knew how hard I had been working.

They wanted to see Clovis have a home as well. I had already been on the phone, texting Randy at work about the entire morning. I texted him, "SHE LET ME PET HER!" We had a celebratory dinner that evening.

Chapter 14

*"But Jesus looked at them and said to them,
'With men this is impossible, but with God all things are possible.'"*
Matthew 19:26

Now that Clovis had let down her guard and was letting me touch her, I wondered how long it would be before she would succumb to our affections. For the next couple of days, we followed the same routine, sitting on the big board with the towel, luring her with the treat, and gently touching her when she would allow. I began by just petting her with one hand only. I thought if I lifted both hands to her, it might be a bit too much. One time I did try to put both my hands on her head and neck, and she pulled away. "Not yet, Mom!" It didn't take long for her to desire more. By Wednesday, December 8th, she was letting me rub her back, all the way down to her tail, with only one hand at first, but by the end of the day, she was allowing me to rub her more vigorously and with both hands. She wasn't sure yet about actually lying down and letting me pet her, but she would stand there, next to me as I sat on the board, and let me stroke her fur down her back. It was as though she wanted to be able to make a quick escape just in case.

I could clearly see her markings—the markings of a Ridgeback. She had no cuts or wounds on her back. It was all fur, running in the opposite direction, characteristic of this breed. I was so relieved! She let me examine her back fairly closely as I pet her, and I saw no sign of a cut, scrape, or wound where we had originally assumed she was injured. Amazing!

After loving on her for two to three minutes, she would back up as if to say, "I need a break. I'm still not sure what's going on here. I'm enjoying it, but I need a minute!" So, I would let her have her space. By the next day, Clovis was lying down and resting by my side, allowing me to pet her almost without limits on time. She was enjoying it without a doubt!

Now that she had stopped running, she could experience all that Randy and I had to give her. God does the same for us if we will just stop running from Him. Our pastor, Robert Morris, said:

"A lot of people are running from God.
It's not His judgment chasing after you;
it's His goodness and mercy. You need to know that the goodness
and mercy of God have been chasing you your whole life.
If you stop running, His goodness and mercy will tackle you!"

Now that Clovis had stopped running, our love and kindness were about to tackle her as well!

Within a couple of days, Clovis had totally surrendered to our touch. I was now taking my big blanket over to the field, spreading it out on the ground so we would have a place to sit together. She came running when she saw me! Randy would go with me when he was home and available but was standing back a few steps, giving her space to feel safe. We didn't want her to think we were ganging up on her.

I would sit on the blanket, and Clovis finally laid down and looked like she was smiling. She not only let me scratch her head, neck, and back, but she rolled over and bared her tummy to me! Yes, she was captivated by how this all felt. All I could think of was that this was all new to her. She had feelings she had never probably had or could remember.

I rubbed her belly and gave her so much attention. She just laid there, totally submissive to me, not scared in the least bit. I tried leaning down to snuggle her near her face, but she withdrew somewhat. Not quite ready for that face-to-face snuggle. I never thought about the fact that she might snap at me. She had shown no signs of doing any such thing. This was a first for her. Everything was a first. I felt confident it would only be another day before she would let me closer. I so wanted to put my face next to hers and cuddle. She was so sweet and gentle. I couldn't imagine that she wouldn't want to cuddle me right back!

With all the excitement and petting going on, we decided to take a video of her reaction to me. The next time we walked over, I used my phone to video her running up to me, tail wagging, tongue hanging out in anticipation of a treat. I almost thought she would jump up on me and knock me down. She was elated! Next, I walked over to the treat board, passing the phone to Randy so he could video Clovis allowing me to pet her. And boy did she! I sat on the board for several minutes, talking to her and scratching anywhere she would allow.

If anyone drove by, they would never believe that this dog had been the stray they had seen for months. She was head over heels with us. I knew right then that it would be only days before she would follow us across the street to our home. Some people wondered why we didn't just grab her and take her home. Why allow her to live outside alone night after night, risking the weather and predators? We knew that Clovis would be OK. She had survived all these years, so a few more days were going to be fine. The weather was cooperating with us. Lows in the 40s and highs upwards of 80 on some days. She could handle that quite well. I kept an eye on the weather predictions just in case, but it looked like smooth sailing for the next couple of weeks. I was trying not to rush her. We never had; why start now? What would she think if we tried to grab her? I never wanted her to feel caught. It was finally apparent that she was falling in love with us too.

Sitting there on the construction lot, petting Clovis and talking to her was such a thrill! I had waited months to touch her, pet her, and let her know that we were trustworthy and would be good to her, and now it was all happening. She not only rolled over and bared her belly, but she also stretched out her back legs and let me scratch every part of her body. She was moving around so I could get to other places on her. "Scratch here, Mom! I want you to pet me over here too!" I could almost hear her saying that. If I stopped petting her for even a second, her right paw would start swiping at me as if to say, "Hey, why'd ya stop? Keep petting me, Mom!" I did, of course! It was so cute the way she would look up at me, thinking I was leaving. Whenever I would halt the petting, her leg would lift up towards me, pawing in the air as if to beg for more. She would get what I call the "crazy eyes" looking at me—eyes full of excitement. She was experiencing a little taste of Heaven!

While I was petting her, I had plenty of time to examine her body. I never had any thoughts of picking up a disease or even getting fleas from her. To my surprise, Clovis had NO fleas! She didn't have a single tick or other bug anywhere on her. How could that be? I never found a scratch or scrape either. All those thorny vines and briars in the woods and yet no indication she had ever been cut or punctured. I was at least expecting to find a scratch somewhere, but no. And I looked everywhere. I searched every inch of that girl's body and found no evidence of any harm whatsoever. It truly was miraculous!

The last thing to examine was her left front paw.

Surprisingly she let me pick it up and look more closely at it. It didn't appear to cause her pain when I touched it. I saw no scabs, cuts, bleeding, or any sign of a trauma that was recent. Nor were there signs of any infections. Her paw was simply—gone. The bulk of her left front paw was missing. Was this from being caught in a trap possibly? It looked more like a birth defect to me. While she was missing part of the paw, she had a couple of pads on the bottom, although they weren't in the right place. If her paw had been trapped and cut off, those pads wouldn't have been in those spots. It looked like something she maybe had always had. I would have to wait for confirmation from a vet once we were able to get her to one. At least I could see there was no imminent danger that needed treatment.

Later that day, I decided I needed to post the videos we took to *Nextdoor* so that all my friends and neighbors who were following the story could see the progress and rejoice with us. We had hundreds of views and responses, which were positive and uplifting. As I knew might happen on social media, we had the naysayers feel the need to express their disdain for our methods:

"Please just put a trap out and get that poor girl! Don't let her spend another night out there!"

And after that one,

"For the love of God, would someone PLEASE catch this dog and give her a home by Christmas?"

People have varying opinions—on everything. Even on topics or situations that they know nothing about. I had to keep reminding myself of that. These negative comments were coming from people who thought they knew better.

They probably assumed that it was much easier to catch her than it was. They had no comprehension of everything we were doing to give her a home by Christmas. Thankfully, most comments were positive and uplifting, even defending Randy and me for our methods. Those who had seen Clovis or been watching my attempts understood. The only thing that should have mattered was that we were going to have her soon.

Still, the hateful, hurtful comments penetrated my mind, and it was hard to let them go. I finally deleted the post that same day. I had wanted people to see Clovis' joy and enthusiasm in coming to me. But those few comments that undercut my mission stung deeply. I couldn't stand to see them anymore.

Fortunately, I also received several private messages of "great job Stacie" reflections. One opened my eyes to see that not only was this journey changing things in me, but it was reaching others in ways I would never dream. I received a message from a woman in Grapevine that meant more to me than anything up to this point:

"Dear Stacie,

I saw your video a little while ago. I was so touched by Clovis and you. I lost my daughter to cancer in August 2020. The grief of losing her is ongoing and so difficult. Words are confusing, and feelings are as well. Seeing you and Clovis together, especially her running towards you, was overwhelmingly beautiful. I saw joy. Love is patient. Love is kind'. Earlier I was hoping I could save the video; seeing you and Clovis helped me let go of the grip of grief and embrace the wonders of 'feelings' and how they can move you. There is truth in a moment. There can be joy in remembering. I guess my job now is accepting that. Your journey with Clovis and now her coming home to you and your husband for this season of the Christmas holidays is a lovely message of hope and contentment. Thank you, Stacie."

Tears welled up in my eyes as I read her beautiful message. Sadly, I had removed the post before she had a chance to save the video. I immediately wrote back, sending her the videos, hoping they could continue to bring her the joy that she needed.

She and I have kept in touch since that second week of December and have plans to meet soon. I would love nothing more than to be able to take Clovis to see her one day. Clovis' story was reaching much further than I ever anticipated. Randy and I knew that if we were going to be able to get Clovis to our home soon and possibly to see my new friend, she would need to be more comfortable with him first.

Within a day or so, Randy was still coming with me, this time with a treat in his hand. It was time to see if she would allow him to pet her. We needed to have her comfortable with both of us.

Clovis would come running to me and sit on the blanket, letting me pet her. Randy would stand back a few feet, kneeling on one knee, and hold out a treat. At first, she wouldn't go to him, so I would get up, go to Randy and sit beside him.

"Come on over, Clovis. It's OK! Look, Randy is a good boy and wants to give you a treat!" She would hop up and come over, a little hesitant, but she trusted me. Randy held the treat out, and Clovis would stop just short of taking it from him. We tried to wait patiently but realized she wasn't ready to grab it from his hand, so I would then take the treat from Randy and hand it to her. We played this little game for a day or two until she finally realized that Randy was a "good boy." She was still a bit shy with Randy, but as long as I was there with him, she would eat from his hand. Success!

After having success with the treats, we wanted to see if she would let Randy pet her. As I had done a few days before, he held out a treat, and as she came to get it, he slowly moved his hand and began to pet her head. As long as I was there, Clovis was fine with it. We continued this routine for a couple of days until Clovis was more used to Randy up close. She knew who he was as he had gone over with me innumerable times over the months, but she was now comfortable with his touch. She knew she had found another friend, her daddy.

The more Clovis let me pet her, the more I could investigate. Next, her teeth and ears. Was it too soon to try to check? I certainly didn't want to scare her. But by Sunday the 12th, I was checking those too. Her ears? Clean as a whistle! No dirt, no mites—nothing! And her teeth? Pearly white and clean as can be. What? A dog who has been out on her own for three years, eating who knows what and having no care has teeth like this? Every day continued to amaze me.

The final thing I noticed while petting her? This little girl had zero odor. She didn't smell like a dog. She didn't smell at all! I rubbed my hands all over her, then turned to Randy, who was nearby. "Smell my hands!" I put my hands under his nose, and he couldn't believe it either. Was it just us? Had I gotten so used to her that I just didn't notice? I ran home and called Sydney. "Sydney, smell my hands!" She looked at me with quite a strange face, and then I explained to her why the odd request. She smelled and said, "Mom, I barely smell anything. There is a bit of odor, but she doesn't smell." The next afternoon, I had been across the street petting Clovis when one of Randy's clients pulled into our driveway. I went back home to talk to her and said, "Pamela, smell my hands!" She looked at me with glaring eyes, wondering what I was talking about. I told her about getting to pet Clovis, and she was so excited too! She smelled my hands and couldn't believe there was no smell—none at all. It's a good thing we have known Pamela for so many years. She, being an animal lover herself, knew all too well the excitement that this day had brought to us.

All my dog dreams were coming true. Not only was Clovis a sweet girl, but she didn't yip and bark constantly. She was healthy as could be, and she didn't smell. Oh, and one more little thing; she barely shed any fur. If I scratched her vigorously enough, sure, she shed some of her fur. But unlike our cat, Thomas, or Natalie's dog, Bodie, Clovis barely let loose any fur.

She was my dream dog! Now to just get her to my home. I assumed she was ready to have a home with us, but it was still tougher than I had anticipated. Every day for the next week, I would visit her, but she would stay near her bed or on the lot. She was letting me hug her at this point, although not for too long. She didn't seem to mind her face right up to mine. She was feeling comfortable and loved. Why won't she just follow me across the street? I would go back home and sit on my porch as I had been doing for months.

Maybe if she continues to see me there, she will finally give in. But no. She would stay put right where she had been comfortable for several weeks now. I was frustrated, mainly because I didn't understand. I wanted her to be with us all the time. Why didn't she want to?

Every day I would go to see her, and she would be waiting for me. The minute I opened my front door, she would come running to greet me. And still, she wouldn't cross the street to our house, which we always found odd. She crossed the street at night to our house as we had seen her on camera for months. Why wouldn't she come during the day? We could never figure that out, but for now, at least she was letting us come to her and lay down with her. Daily for the next week, I would go over and lie down with her. Sometimes on the towel, sometimes back on her mound. The construction workers were watching this in amazement! They had seen this play out during the last month, and now, here I was, sitting back on the mound with her, petting her.

One afternoon that week, while lying on a blanket with Clovis over on the construction lot, I saw my neighbors, Jonathon and Susan, coming down the street, walking their dog, Runway. They caught sight of us and stopped on the road, about 25-30 yards away. They were walking Runway past our house, but upon seeing Clovis lying with me, they decided not to disturb us. They stopped and watched for a while, with Runway wanting to explore and see who this new dog was. Clovis just watched. Up to this point, she had never responded to another dog, and that day was no different.

I always assumed she did this to not draw attention to herself. Whatever the reason, she didn't act very interested in Runway. Maybe someday, they would be friends! The following day, I went to the mailbox to find a card and a Petsmart gift card from Jonathan and Susan. How sweet and thoughtful! We have such great neighbors and friends who cared about Clovis. I was anxious to be able to use the gift card to buy Clovis her first collar, tag, or leash.

The following day, we had yet another surprise from a neighbor. 7:00 am had been breakfast call all year, and it was no different now. Our daily routine had become known somewhat to the neighborhood. I would fix her food, head out the door, and go to the lot.

She would come running to greet me halfway, and I would take her food back to her bed and sit with her while she ate.

If I had time and didn't need to get to work, I would stay longer. Most days, however, I would visit with her and pet her for a few minutes before needing to get home. One morning, after I had dropped off her breakfast and returned home, I fixed my breakfast and took it outside to sit on the glider on the front porch so I could watch her. A car pulled up in front of our house and stopped. A woman I didn't recognize got out, and came to the porch carrying a small package. She had tears in her eyes as she began to speak:

"I just wanted to bring this to you. I was going to drop it off, but I saw you sitting out here, and I wanted to give it directly to you. My name is Penny Ledbetter, and our family lives around the corner. We have been watching you for a long time now, trying to get that stray dog, and today, my husband was on his way to work. When he was coming up to your house, he saw the dog over on the right side of the street running towards the road. He looked to the left and saw you walking out with a bowl of food. He called me immediately from his car and said, 'Penny, you won't believe what I just saw!' He told me she was running towards you, tail wagging and coming to you for food. We are so happy!"

Penny and I talked for quite awhile about Clovis' story and it was so heart-warming to see how the saga had touched her family's lives. Penny, as others had also told me, remarked, "Stacie, you've been acting towards Clovis the way God acts towards us. You've been so patient and compassionate. Just how the Lord is to us!" We never knew it, but she said that many nights they would talk at the dinner table about the dog and how we were trying to win her over. They had seen her on multiple occasions and watched our story unfold. She brought us the sweetest card. On the envelope, it just said, "Sweet neighbor." The card read, "With God, all things are possible." Matthew 19:26. She had written on the inside:

"Dear neighbor,

We have LOVED witnessing you patiently love and care for the beautiful stray dog. We are in awe of how you never gave up. Love, the Ledbetter family."

Along with the card, she had several dog biscuits wrapped up for Clovis. My heart was so touched by this gesture from an unknown neighbor. I knew that neighbors were following the story, but this was evidence of that.

People watch our behaviors. They see what we are doing. It seemed the whole neighborhood was keeping track of Clovis' tale. Penny and I continued to talk for quite a while that morning as I filled her in on our sweet Clovis. To see another woman, who I had not known before, react to our story the way she did, gave me assurance that we had done the right thing. We had been patient. We had been compassionate. Most of all, we had not given up.

Chapter 15

"I will both lie down in peace, and sleep; For You alone, O Lord, make me dwell in safety."

Psalms 4:8

Nine days had passed since Clovis first let me pet her. Every day since then only brought her closer and closer to us. She was always eagerly waiting for one of us to come out our front door and head over to see her. Tail wagging, head bouncing up and down, she would come running. Then stop. It was almost as if there was an invisible barrier between the lot across the street and the road. We contemplated not going over to see her just to see if she would make her way over to our home, but she was stubborn. She wanted things on her timeline just as we had always done.

During all this time, with the new construction of all three houses across from us, we met our new neighbors that lived directly across the street from us and adjacent to Clovis' lot. Rick and Terri Urbanek, who live part-time in Wichita Falls due to work, had become familiar with our story of Clovis. Rick and Terri have two dogs and wanted to see Clovis find a home with us. Terri makes all of her dog food, something I thought that I would never do. It was about this time that Terri gave me a day's serving of her special homemade, all organic, all-natural, made with love dog food! One Ziploc bag of the food was a serving size for a dog of Clovis' size, but I wanted that food to last. I was going to use it as bribery! Every meal, I would sprinkle a little bit of Terri's food on top of the dry food I was feeding Clovis. It had to have been like a drug to Clovis! I was desperate and hoped that anything new and tasty might get her to follow me home across the street.

Because Rick and Terri live part-time in another city, they had not been around for these days that Clovis had allowed us to pet her. When

153

they pulled into their driveway one afternoon, we were sitting outside on a blanket with Clovis next to their driveway. Terri got so emotional and teary-eyed. She was extremely happy to see the progress we had made. We appreciated the food she had given us and continued to give us during the following weeks. I used it sparingly, leaving it more of a dessert for Clovis.

Speaking of dessert, one afternoon, while going to see Clovis, I unwrapped one of the dog biscuits that Penny and Lane had given us. They were about 4" long and shaped like a dog bone. I was anxious to see how Clovis would like them! I went to see her, sat on my towel, and petted her for a while before giving her the biscuit. Once I held it out, she snatched it away and ran off! I watched her run about 20 yards away from me, and she began to dig. She was furiously digging a hole and then dropped the biscuit right inside. Using her nose, she covered it all back up. Me, not ever having dogs before, found this fascinating! Did she not like it? I know my cats will paw over things that they don't like. If I give them food in their bowl that they find unsavory, they will take their paw and mimic covering it up as they do their poo in the litter box.

The vet told me that's why they do that! They want to let you know they equate the food to being as tasty as their poo. Was this what Clovis thought? Or did she find this treat so new and wonderful that she was hiding it, saving it for later? I had never seen her bury a treat before. I had no idea what it all meant at the time, but she seemed to know what she was doing. Later, as she would bury every single biscuit I gave her, I read that dogs bury their favorite treats to save. With Clovis having been out on her own for so long, maybe this was a way to store food from other critters for safekeeping.

Every day seemed to be something new or fun with Clovis. On Wednesday, I got a text from Randy while he was at work:

"I'm at Tom Thumb Grocery Store while I have a break, and they have dog collars and leashes on sale. Do you want me to get one for Clovis?"

"Yes! Pick out whatever you want!"

Later that afternoon, when he got home, we were excited to take it over to Clovis and see if she would let us put it on her. I sat down on the board where we always met, talked to her a bit and petted her, then explained to her what was about to happen:

"Clovis, daddy got you this pretty collar! I'm going to put it on you because we want people to know you are loved and safe and belong to someone." She sat so still while I put the collar on.

Piece of cake! She didn't seem to mind in the least. We were able to go home that afternoon, feeling a little better about her being out there. Now, at least if someone saw her, they would know she belonged to someone. I only wish the coyotes knew! Once again, that night, while I was sleeping, I heard Clovis bark. Just one single bark. I peeked out the blinds again, facing the east side of the house since that is where the sound came from. I looked out to see a coyote running behind our carport and into the woods. Clovis had done her job of scaring him away. I found it so funny that after only hearing her bark once on Thanksgiving Day, I could identify her bark, even in my sleep. Once I realized that Clovis was again safe, I drifted off back to sleep.

The following day, Randy and I headed off to Petsmart to use the gift card that Jonathan and Susan had given us. We already knew the first thing we needed was a tag. We picked out a pretty silver and pink, bone-shaped tag that looked like something a little girl dog should have on. Engraved on one side, CLOVIS. On the other side, it simply said, "MY PARENTS" and then listed our address and phone numbers. We felt some comfort, even though we didn't believe anyone else would ever actually pick her up. She belonged to us now. At least that's what it felt like. We thought about attaching the leash and trying to get her to come with us, but something inside me said, "No. It's too soon. Just wait." It made me a bit unsettled, but so far, all the decisions we had made had worked out. So, the leash would have to wait.

Now that I had observed Clovis up close and knew that she was at least part Rhodesian Ridgeback, I ventured home to read up on the breed. So much was making sense now! What I read about them said that they are very protective of loved ones and extremely, meltingly affectionate with the ones they trust. Clovis was proving overly affectionate with me now that she knew she could trust me completely. I never imagined that after only a couple of days of touching her that she would let me so freely pet and stroke her entire body. I also found that Ridgebacks have a quiet, gentle temperament and rarely bark. Ah! To this point, I had only heard her bark three times—in a year!

While they can appear big and lazy like a hound at times, they can be a threatening presence in that while they are not barkers, they are alert watchdogs, alerting their loved ones to anything unusual. And finally, I discovered this: Ridgebacks are extremely clean dogs with a slight odor and minimal shedding. TRUE. TRUE. And TRUE!

As the week continued, Randy and I began talking about how we might get her to cross the street to our house on her own.

We could try the leash, but we had no idea what she had been through in the past. Maybe a leash would frighten her or remind her of some type of abuse. So, we decided to continue to be patient. The week of December 13-18 was unusually warm for winter weather. Lows were in the 60s and highs up to 78. This was perfect because we had plenty of nice weather to sit outside and coax her over. Plus, there was no need to worry about cold, freezing temperatures at night. We tried sitting out on our porch, walking over to see her, bringing treats of every kind, including Terri's famous dog food.

Nothing was getting through. She would run from her bed to the last couple of feet of the lot before reaching the street and sit down. There was a row of small bushes along the road that she would lie behind. It was as if there was an invisible fence at the edge of the lot, preventing her from crossing the street. She would watch us from the bushes, assuming that she was hidden from us.

Finally, on the evening of the 16th, Randy and I walked over once more to see her. When we were done petting her and talking with her, we finally tried the leash.

She didn't mind us putting it on the collar, but she immediately laid down and wouldn't budge. We tried to get her to stand up at least, but no. She would have nothing to do with moving. If we wanted her to move, she would lay there like a rock. We looked at each other, knowing it just wasn't time yet, and we didn't want to try to force her to come with us. So, we took the leash off and decided to walk back home. We turned to leave, me walking ahead of Randy. As we got to the street, ready to cross, we could hear her behind us. I knew if I turned to look at her, she would stop. "Keep walking, Stacie." I thought to myself. I began crossing the street while Randy followed. I reached our yard and heard Randy from behind me say, "Stacie, she's following us!"

"Keep walking, Randy. Don't look back."

We got to the yard, turned to sit in the grass, and she had crossed the street! She came into the yard but stopped about 5 yards away from the road.

She sat there looking at us. We began talking to her: "Clovis, you came over! Come here, girl. We want to pet you and love on you! Why don't you come sit with us?"

She approached slowly, then turned and ran back to her construction lot home. SO CLOSE! We wondered what it was going to take but also realized that this entire process had been one step at a time. The darkness was approaching, so we decided to go on inside ourselves, knowing that Clovis had already had her dinner and the weather was beautiful. She would be alright for another night.

December, the 17th came and went as usual for a regular Friday workday. I made my usual visits to see Clovis, and it was so nice now. She was always happy to see me and ready for a bit of snuggling.

Every day she was becoming more at ease. I could now place both my hands on her face or neck and put my face next to hers to give her a kiss on the top of her head. She wasn't afraid of that anymore. I could tell she enjoyed it! If I removed my hands, she would swipe a paw at me again as if to say, "Keep doing that, mommy."

That afternoon, we were watching the weather. Storms were predicted with heavy rains and possible hail. I couldn't stand the thought of her being out there! The storms didn't look like they would hit until the middle of the night, but I wanted to get things ready for her. I took another old blanket, along with a treat, and headed over to see Clovis around 4:00 pm. Of course, she came running to me as usual. I took the blanket and went inside the new house. Because of construction delays, it still had no windows or doors. Luckily, it had the roof now. I took the blanket into the large garage and spread it out, placing the treat on top.

I called Clovis in, and surprisingly she came to me inside the house. She had been in the house before, cutting through to escape me in the past, but this was the first time I ever saw her go into something and stay.

We sat there for a moment, and she had her treat. I stayed with her for a few minutes and then explained to her, fully believing she knew I was saying, "Clovis, there's going to be some storms tonight. I want you to be safe and dry, so you come in here if it starts to get bad, OK?" She looked at me with those beautiful brown eyes as though she understood. I was hoping she knew what I was telling her.

That afternoon, because Randy and I had finished work early for the day, we headed out for our usual Friday night pizza date. Like most nights that we would go out, as soon as we were done eating, one of us would say,

"Is there anything you want to go do?" To which the other usually replied, "Not really." Of course, we both knew what we wanted to do: Get home to Clovis! Not that Randy and I had ever been much for grand social events or going out, but it was even worse now. We just wanted to be home, watching, praying for, feeding, and now petting Clovis. As usual, we rushed home to see her. It was now about 5:30 pm, and we headed over to see our girl. She popped up from her bed and ran to greet us across the street but stopping shy of the road. She laid down, wanting us to sit and pet her where she was. She didn't want to come with us at first.

After a few minutes of loving on her, Randy and I decided to again, walk back across the street to see if she would follow us. As we crossed the street, we could sense that she was behind us. Randy called to me, "She's coming, Stacie." We kept walking until we reached our yard, spread out a blanket, and sat down in the grass. This time, she approached us! We began to pet and scratch her belly. It was like a picture out of a Hallmark movie. Mom, Dad, and Clovis all lying in the yard, enjoying the evening. We sat there with her, just petting her and talking to her until it started to get darker.

Because it was December, the sun was down fairly quickly, and it was completely dark by 6:30. We weren't sure what to do. I asked Randy, "What should we do? Do we just get up and go inside? Do we stay out here as long as she wants us to?"

We decided to take what we had left of the bale of straw and spread some in a couple of places near our house and backyard. We also put blankets out with the straw, trying to mimic her bed on the mound. Randy also has a workshop out in the backyard attached to our gym. We left the door of the workshop open, with a blanket inside. Maybe, just maybe, she would go inside out of the storms if they did come. I had doubts, but at least it was there. We were hoping she might decide to stay the night, but I was sure she wouldn't feel very safe out in the open, closer to coyote land. I was even more sure that she wouldn't go into Randy's workshop. To Clovis, that screamed "TRAP!" When we were done fixing the beds, we talked to Clovis and beckoned her to follow us around the west side of the house and into the yard. The chain-link fence has four gates, and we began walking toward the back gate. She amazingly followed us. To our surprise, she came right into our backyard as well! Randy and I sat out in the back, again just petting her and trying to make her feel relaxed. We showed her two different beds we had set up for her within the fenced yard, as well as a water bowl and a treat. We continued to sit with her until almost 8:00 pm, and we were clueless as to what to do next. We would have to go inside to bed ourselves soon, but what about Clovis?

Do we close the gate, thereby locking her in and possibly terrifying her? Would she be more at risk to coyotes, unable to get out of the yard if they came to attack? Or would she be in a panic and cause damage to herself or the fence while trying to get out? Randy wasn't in agreement with me at first, but then he gave in: we would go inside to sleep but leave Clovis in the backyard with the gate open. We knew it was a risk. We knew she would probably leave. But I also knew that she would probably come back the next day. She trusted us. She was beginning to love us. She didn't want to lose her newfound family. The last thing I wanted was for her to find herself locked up in a yard with no way out. Randy and I headed back inside after telling her goodnight and said a quick prayer over her for peaceful sleep. I had almost forgotten about the coming storms.

Randy and I enjoyed the rest of the evening and then headed off to bed. It was a short sleep as the rain woke me. It was howling outside! The rain was crashing down so hard, beating against the bedroom windows.

I knew that rain couldn't hurt her, but to be sitting out there in it, alone, in the dark—I couldn't stand it!

We peeked out in the back, and of course, she had gone. It was no surprise to me, but I wondered where she had gone to take refuge from the storm. So, at 3:00 am, I said to Randy, "I have to go check on her. I need to see where she is." I slipped on some clothes, put on my mud shoes, grabbed my coat and umbrella, flashlight, and a treat, and headed over to the construction lot.

The rain was really coming down! As I walked through the lot toward the garage, my feet sank into the mud. I finally reached the garage, and when I looked inside, she was there! I could not believe it! She remembered the blanket and where we had been sitting and returned to find shelter from the rain. To my knowledge, this was the first time she had done anything like this.

As I approached and called her name, she lit up like a Christmas tree. I swear she smiled at me while her tail started swinging 90 mph. I went over to her, sat down on the blanket, and just stroked her fur. "Clovis, you're such a good girl! And you remembered the blanket I put out here for you. You're such a smart girl!" I must have sat with her for 15-20 minutes, contemplating lying down and sleeping with her, but then I came to my senses. I knew she was safe. I knew she was dry. And I knew she would be out of the hail. Clovis had come so far, trusting that the shelter was safe. Did she trust it because she knew I put it there for her?

Whatever the reason, she was safe.

As I got up to leave, Clovis stayed lying on the blanket as if she knew I wanted her to remain inside the garage for the night. I went home, beaming from ear to ear.

"Randy! She was in the garage on the blanket!" It was difficult for me to go back to sleep; I was so excited. But soon, it would hit me how tired I was, and I knew that morning was coming soon. Thank goodness it would be Saturday morning, and I would not have to be ready for work. I wondered if she would still be there the next morning.

The following day, we awoke to an empty backyard. It didn't shock me since I knew she had left before the storm. I expected it. I also knew where she would be. Yes, she was waiting for me over on the mound. I'm sure she stayed on her blanket in the garage as long as she needed, but once the rain stopped, she must have gone back to her haven. Once she saw me open our front door, she came rather quickly to greet me! This time, she crossed the street all on her own and followed us right back to our backyard.   Clovis stayed all day in our yard, letting us pet her and play with her. We were elated! As nighttime approached, we decided to close the gate. We had the two beds made for Clovis, one right up next to the house in case she felt safer with a wall of protection behind her, and one right off our patio, surrounded on one side with bushy plants that might give her a sense of being hidden. She chose the bed by the plants, and off to sleep she went.

I messaged our neighbor, Jonathan, and his wife, Susan,

"Hey Jonathan, Clovis has a nice bed in the back with the wind blocked and a bed in the warmer shed if she'll just go in. Beverly is going to come tomorrow, and once we determine if Clovis has no fleas, etc., we will let her come in our sunroom if she wants to," I wrote.

He replied, "You closed the gate tonight?"

"YES! And she seems fine! I actually went out at 3:00 am last night in the rain to make sure she had found her bed that I put in the new house—and she was there—so out of the rain," I replied.

"She was in the yard all last night?" he asked.

"No, she went out the gate and across the street. I had made her a bed inside that new house in case of rain. She was there when I went to check on her. But she came over this morning and has been in the yard all day," I wrote.

"You're going to heaven for sure," Jonathan replied.

"Ha-ha. I feel like God put this little girl in my path for sure!" I said.

"I hope by next Christmas you can share a picture like this!"

Sharing a picture with me, Jonathan had sent me a sweet shot of Runway, lying on his dog bed, covered in a blanket, lying by the Christmas tree.

"Oh, my goodness! I hope it's by this Christmas! We decided to try to let her sleep in our sunroom tonight because we just started to worry about her. But she won't come in. She came to the door and sniffed but then ran out and laid back down in her bed in the yard.

"Randy will sleep in the sunroom so that he is close by and can see/hear. She should be warm enough where she is, but it's her first night. I started worrying about her, and then I have to remember she has been out in far worse conditions for the last two to three years," I replied.

Jonathan closed with, "Think what she dealt with last February! You have gotten where you are with baby steps. I think she will be in your sunroom soon. Maybe bring a bed or blanket she is familiar with into the sunroom. Amazing how far she has come in two weeks. Really nice that Randy will be there for her."

The next morning, we awoke to find our sweet little Clovis lying on her bed, waiting for us to come out. She wasn't eating much right now, but we assumed it might just be from stress or anxiety. She was now in a new yard, with a new bed and completely new surroundings. But she wanted to be with us. Clovis was still enjoying her treats, but her food went untouched. That's OK. I tried to tell myself. She will eat when she gets hungry and feels more comfortable. Besides, she must be feeling more peaceful. I had always been concerned for her mental health—always running, always having to be on alert. But now, in our yard, I was hoping she could finally find peace while she slept. Her appetite would return soon, I was sure.

Around 9:00 am, I received a text from Jonathan:

"How did she do?"

"She did great! Randy said he must have looked out there 50 times, and she was always curled up on her blanket. She hasn't acted like she wants to get out of the fence. She lays on the patio or close to it, staring at the sunroom doors. She doesn't want to come in yet, but I bet it won't be long! She hasn't eaten yet, and I don't know if she's just nervous, but she doesn't seem interested in eating. Thank you for checking on her!" I replied.

Then around 2:00 pm:

"Any luck getting her inside?" Jonathan texted.

"She cautiously came in the back doors to get a treat and then ran outside. I have learned the way this has been going that she will be in by tomorrow at the latest! Hopefully, by tonight though. It's like once she makes that first step, then it really doesn't take that much longer now," I wrote back.

"Has Beverly stopped by?" (Referring to our neighbor, the vet), Jonathan asked.

"No, not yet. She said sometime this afternoon. I'm anxious to see if Clovis will let her look at her," I wrote.

"Too bad it's cold out. I wonder what would happen if you left your door open?" he replied.

(It was too chilly to leave our back door standing open, but not too cold out yet for a dog).

He went on, "Have any 'strangers' tried to meet her?"

I replied, "Not in the last day or so. It's strange because she seems to know the people in the neighborhood. For instance, if you walked by, it wouldn't scare her. She might not let you pet her, but she wouldn't growl because she recognizes you. My daughter, who lives in Grapevine, came over a few days ago and went with me to see her across the street. Clovis growled at her! I've never heard her do that. I think she might have just been protective of me, not knowing Natalie. And we are going to keep trying to get her into our sunroom today. But just like everything else we have done, we want her to take the lead on that. Maybe you all should come down later and see how she responds to you!"

3:50 pm:

"Can I walk down?" texted Jonathan.

"Sure! Come to the back by the gym," I closed.

Jonathan came by and visited with Clovis over the fence. As he stood at the chain-linked fence, Clovis was sticking by my side like peanut butter on bread. She wouldn't budge! As long as I was there, Clovis seemed OK with Jonathan talking to us. She was trembling a little, her body quivering just a tad, but otherwise, she was fine. We spoke with him for a good while, and a few others approached. Julie and her daughter, Olivia, happened to be taking a walk when they saw us all at the back gate with Clovis. They slowly came closer and asked if it was OK. I felt confident that Clovis would be familiar with Julie, having lived partly in her yard for the last year. Again, Clovis didn't seem unusually upset. She laid next to me, letting me pet her the entire time we spoke. She was nervous, but I figured if she was really scared, she would have run to the other side of the yard to escape all the people. Finally, while everyone was still there, Beverly, the veterinarian, walked up. I think it was all a bit too much for Clovis. She was still lying beside me, but she was getting anxious, trembling more now. Jonathan, Julie, and Olivia all decided it was best to leave us alone, but Beverly stayed for a few minutes to give Clovis a look over from the gate. She wasn't ready to come in and examine Clovis yet. She wanted her to become familiar with her first. From where she was standing, Beverly thought she looked fairly healthy. She estimated, from what I told her of her clean teeth, that she probably wasn't over five years old, but again, we had no idea. We did discover a remarkable surprise: Clovis had been spayed! We wondered why she had never had a litter of pups out there.

We don't get many stray dogs in our area, and almost everyone has their dog leashed. But to live outside for three years and NOT get pregnant was miraculous.

Now we knew why. We pondered what her story was. Had she been someone's pet? Had she been in a shelter and been spayed and then, when adopted, got loose?

Shelters will give the animals a tattoo on their belly to show they have been spade, but Clovis didn't have one. We figured we would never know her backstory.

I'm not sure I wanted to know. We made plans to have Beverly return at a later day to let Clovis become familiar with her. I was anxious to see what, if anything, Clovis would need, but after three years, another week or two wouldn't hurt.

The afternoon went on smoothly, the hours filled with just sitting with Clovis and reassuring her that we were her family now.

Around 6:20, on the second night of sleeping in our yard, just as it had gotten dark and we had gone inside for dinner, Randy happened to see Clovis frantically trying to dig out from under the fence! Before he knew it, she was outside the fence and running. Panic struck us at first. She was not necessarily running FROM us, but we were worried that she might revert back to her behavior from months ago. Did she have some kind of traumatic experience and was feeling the need to escape once again?

I quickly picked up my phone and once again texted Jonathan:

"She just dug out from the fence and left!"

"Curious if she went across the street ... Be patient. She knows you have a great home for her," he replied.

Jonathan knew just what to say. He had been so helpful along the way, and I needed someone's reassurance right now besides Randy. Randy always had my back, but I needed to know from another dog owner that everything would be alright and that our approach with Clovis was OK. So many times, I would hear comments from others, usually on social media, about what was taking us so long or why we "didn't do this or that," and I would begin to doubt my tactics. Jonathan was reaffirming my ways.

I responded, "I am over here now at the lot and don't see her. I'll put her blankets back over here in case she sleeps here again. I'm not scared she ran away. I just hope she doesn't run out into the street in a frantic mess!"

My words were, unfortunately, prophetic. We had quickly gone outside to call for her. I assumed she would go back across the street to her bed on the mound. As I shined the flashlight around the lot, looking for her but not seeing her, Randy and I turned and looked back towards our house across the street. She was still in the field on the west side of our house, about 20 yards away. She had never really gone that far! Then, without thinking, I shined the light at her and hollered, "Clovis!!" She saw me and started to RUN to me—right across the street! At that exact moment, a car was coming, and I had to close my eyes and turn my head away, too scared to watch. It looked for sure like she was going to get hit. It was dark, and she was hard to see. I screamed, "Clovis, no!" Luckily, she once again avoided being hit. I was shaking, so upset with myself for calling out to her and almost causing her injury. I hadn't thought at all—just reacted. She finally reached me, wagging her tail and acting so joyous. I began to cry as I was not only happy that she was safe but happy that she wanted to be with me. She was excited to see us! I messaged Jonathan one more time to let him know the good news: "She just came running back! We don't have her in the yard yet, but she sure is having fun running around." Randy and I began walking home, and that little girl followed us back and into the yard. We were just glad she returned so quickly. I let Jonathan know:

"She just ran into the backyard and laid down on her blanket. It's almost like she just needed to get out and play a little bit!"

"Maybe she didn't want an audience to poop!" he joked.

Ha-ha! That made me laugh, but maybe he was right! Randy worked briefly on the fence to close the hole she had dug and then decided to sleep in our sunroom once again. The rest of the night, Clovis slept soundly on her new bed. I'm not so sure that Randy did.

The following morning, we all rejoiced that she was still in the yard and happy to see us! Randy reminded me that the 18th of December, the first night she spent the night in our yard, was also his father's birthday. He had passed away a little over two years ago. This small miracle of Clovis finally staying with us through the night on his dad's birthday felt not just like a victory but a memorial.

Chapter 16

*"Every good gift and every perfect gift is from above,
and comes down from the Father of lights …"*

James 1:17

The next few days were so exciting for us all. Clovis was now in our yard every day and every night, and she no longer tried to dig out from under the fence. The reason? She needed to "do her business!" We discovered this the next morning, after her escape on Saturday night. We had noticed that Clovis had not gone to the bathroom in our yard, which we thought was strange since she had now been there about two full days. We talked to Jonathan again and discussed the possibility that maybe she didn't want to go potty in the same area where she was sleeping.

After all, having been out on her own for so long, she probably went elsewhere to do her business to not attract wildlife and critters to her feeding and sleeping area. To test this theory, Randy and I discussed letting her out of the fence to see what she would do. We had no fear that she would run away and never come back.

We didn't know what to expect. We went out to the backyard that Sunday and Clovis ran to the corner gate almost automatically. This was the gate through which we had originally brought her into our yard, so she was familiar with it. We hesitantly opened the gate, and she took off! She ran out into the field and over to the row of trees not far from our home on the west side of the house, about 20 yards away. We watched her scurrying along the tree line, nose down, sniffing away.

All of a sudden, she squatted; that was it! She had to go! No sooner than she had finished, she bolted back to the gate and into the yard. She had no intention of running off. She just wanted her privacy, as Jonathan had amusingly predicted. Later that evening, we witnessed the same thing:

she ran out of the gate as we opened it, explored the woods for about five minutes maximum, and then as soon as she finished going potty, she once again sprinted back into our yard, happy as could be. This truly was remarkable. She didn't want to go potty in our yard and was perfectly happy with being let out, only to return immediately. We continued with this method for about a month, only because she refused to go in the yard, yet she wasn't quite ready for a leash either. She was still resisting the leash, stubbornly lying on the ground without budging every time we tried. We figured it would be fine to let her out in this manner, keeping an eye on her the whole time. She would soon enough feel safe to go in our yard, especially once she began sleeping inside, away from all predators.

For the first week that Clovis was in our backyard, she continued to sleep outside. Thankfully the weather was highly cooperative. Once I realized that Clovis was here to stay, I decided I should venture across the street to pick up her bedding and bowls. I hadn't been back over to the lot, the very lot I had visited multiple times a day for ten months, since the night she first came across to our house, other than when she briefly escaped. As I walked over to the house to pick up the blanket out of the garage, I was suddenly overwhelmed. I can't even say why. I knew that Clovis was now safe. I knew she was now being cared for. I knew she was happy. So, why did I feel so incredibly sad? The tears began to flow, or rather flood, as I saw her large pawprints in the dirt. As I walked around the lot, picking up her things and remembering everything that had taken place over the past ten months, I couldn't help but feel engulfed with emotions. I was happy this quest was finally finished, but the reality of where she had been living, what she had been experiencing, what she had survived, struck me astonishingly hard. I couldn't stop the sobbing. I sat down on the board—the same board where Clovis and I used to meet for treats and continued to cry. It was almost as if I was sad it was over. So confusing! I went back to her bed and sat on the mound. I even walked over to the brushy trash pile where I first sang to her. It all came tumbling down on me like an avalanche of feelings. I wasn't prepared for this at all. I assumed everything would be happy from here on out. All I could reason was that the very thing I had dedicated my life to for the past year was now finished. Yes, Clovis still needed me and would continue to be part of our family, but the work I had put in, the countless hours of work, were now over. Maybe the reality of how she had been living had finally hit me as well. Had the Lord been protecting my feelings so that I could continue on my mission of winning her over without falling victim to my emotions?

For whatever the reason, I wasn't prepared, and I went home feeling completely exhausted. I came in to tell Randy, and he hardly knew what to say. I'm sure he was as surprised as I was by my reaction to seeing the lot across the street. I found Clovis in the yard and continued to cry, telling her how thankful I was that she finally followed us home. I'm sure she could sense my sadness as she lay there, letting me pet her and kiss her on the top of her head.

Once I regained my composure, I knew it was time to let our neighbors know the good news! I headed to the social media site I had used this entire time when discussing Clovis, *Nextdoor*. I posted a couple of photos of Clovis and titled it:

Clovis Now Has a Home!

"Clovis now has a home! Just wanted everyone who had followed this little girl's story the last year to know that she is now in our home, safe and sound! Thanks to all who have inquired about her and even prayed for this poor girl. She seems healthy (for being on her own for two+ years) and will have a vet visit asap. My Christmas present for sure."

The response was overwhelming! Over 600 neighbors read and liked the posting, and over 90 people commented on the story—everything from "My heart is singing" or "This is the best Christmas story ever!" to "This brought tears to my eyes." Everyone was so supportive, so encouraging. The outpouring of love from those I knew and those I didn't was amazing. I soon started a group on *Nextdoor* just for those wanting updates on her condition and her life. So many people joined, asking for pictures and updates from things pertaining to her relationship with the cats to vet appointments and diagnosis of her paw.

It's surprising how a helpless animal can bring an entire community together, bonding over one common love. The love continued to pour in from those we knew, with gifts of dog treats, toys, and even a bed.

On December 23rd, Rick and Terri, our friends across the street, gave us an incredible dog bed for Clovis! We weren't sure what she would think of it. After all, straw, grass, sticks, and dirt had been her "bed" for nearly three years. Would she love it or find it strange? We placed it outside on our patio, just a few feet from the sliding doors, looking into our sunroom. We threw one of her blankets over the top, hoping that would make it more familiar to her. I don't think it mattered. She hopped on that bed and snuggled in as though she were in heaven! From that night on, Clovis slept on her new dog bed, right on the patio.

By the 25th, Christmas Day, we were fantasizing about having her in the house for all the traditional Christmas festivities as we celebrated the birth of Jesus Christ. We pulled her bed into the sunroom, hoping that now that she was used to it, she would come in and lie down on it. Not yet ready. I placed a treat on her bed, and she very cautiously tip-toed into the room, grabbed it, and headed back outside to the porch. She was still cautious as usual. She would approach entering a new room just like she had everything else. Slowly.

We moved the bed back outside for nighttime since she wasn't yet ready to come in to sleep. She was happy enough—this bed was her first real bed, and she was loving it. She would curl up on the blanket every chance she got. Get up to eat? Run back to the bed. Get up to go potty? Run back to the bed. It was as if she had hit the jackpot!

During all this time, our cats, Rocky and Thomas, were wondering who the new visitor to the backyard was. Knowing that Rocky would be the one to protest the loudest, we were so very skeptical of letting him into the sunroom where he could see Clovis. The sunroom is, in actuality, the "cat's room." They laid out there during the day, watching the birds and squirrels through the big picture windows, chattering to them every chance they got.

Their litter box is also in the sunroom, so they migrate towards that room much of the day. We finally let them come into the room, knowing they would go straight to the door to watch Clovis. We were astonished! Thomas wasn't phased one bit. Although he is our extremely skittish cat around people or noises, he is usually calm around other animals. He may not want to play with other animals or snuggle up, but he doesn't run and hide, nor does he hiss or growl. Rocky would be the true test and the one aspect of this entire rescue that would make or break the deal. Rocky, to our surprise, just sat at the window and watched. Oh, he ruffled up his fur and even hissed a time or two, but not his regular growling and moaning as he does when Bodie is over.

He was reacting more like a regular cat. This may not sound earth-shattering, but we were amazed. Completely ready for Rocky to react with ferocious growls and hisses, we anxiously waited to see his response to this new, large creature in "his" yard. But he just sat and watched. Randy and I stared at each other. Could this be God? Had our prayers for our animals been answered? The one thing that we were most worried about from day one was beginning to look like a moot point. It would take Rocky a little time to get completely used to Clovis. Still, by December 26th, on a sunny day in Texas winter, all three animals sat out in the backyard together, watching each other yet leaving one another alone.

Truly miraculous for Rocky! Rocky let out a hiss now and then if Clovis came too close, but in comparison to how he treated Bodie in the past, we were elated.

Realizing that Rocky wasn't going to attack Clovis but was merely wanting to exert his dominance, we decided to try once again to get Clovis to come into the house to sleep. After all, it was December, and the warmer weather wouldn't last forever. On December 29th, she finally made her way, very cautiously, into the sunroom to lay on her bed. She didn't dare venture outside that room and into the rest of the house. The sunroom was as far as she was willing to explore.

Wondering how she would do sleeping in the house—inside a house— for the first time, Randy decided to sleep in the sunroom so that she wouldn't be alone. I'm not sure how well Randy slept, but Clovis was at peace, sleeping without having to worry about outdoor predators or critters who were simply nuisances. The following day, Clovis went back outside to play and rest in the backyard but eagerly came into the sunroom again to sleep at night. That night, I slept in the sunroom with her, giving Randy a much-needed break to get some better rest himself.

As the week went on, Clovis continued to sleep in the sunroom but would finally make her way to the living room. We placed her bed by the sofa so that one of us could sleep there next to her. She didn't explore any of the other rooms of the house. The living room was her haven now. I slept beside her for three nights, just keeping an eye on her, hoping Rocky would leave her alone during the darkness of night. No altercations! It seemed Rocky was ready to ignore Clovis for now.

This new relationship between Clovis and the cats continued to improve over the next few weeks. Rocky was determined to prove his dominance, but he never hurt Clovis. On one occasion, Clovis came a little too close for comfort with a bit of excitement, and Rocky took a swipe at her nose. I heard a yelp from Clovis, but no one was harmed. From that moment on,

Clovis knew that Rocky was not a cat to be messed with. If Rocky walked in the room, Clovis would lie down, put her head down on her paws, and lie perfectly still. Rocky would come up, sniff her body and nose, but Clovis wouldn't budge.

After proving he was king, Rocky would walk on. Rocky had indeed shown Clovis that he would be the boss, he would be the ruler, and he would be in control of his domain. Clovis didn't seem to mind. She stayed out of Rocky's way and always allowed him to have the right of way in a room. Luckily, Thomas was much friendlier and would even jump up on the sofa, close to Clovis. We were overjoyed that Rocky was being this easy-going with Clovis. We had imagined the worst, for some reason not fully believing that God would take care of this, too.

It would be a full month or more before Clovis would let curiosity lead her into our bedroom or other areas of the house. She was still nervous and anxious, but as time went on, she became more and more settled, more and more at home. She eventually began following me from room to room. She had to know where I was at all times. Yes, I was her person. She loved Randy and now Sydney and Mylon too, but it was me that she had to have her eyes on.

I started wondering if I would ever be able to get up without her right on my heels. When I went out to our gym to work, she would follow me outside and sit by the gate closest to the gym door. At first, she would greet all my clients as they arrived but wasn't keen on letting them pet her unless I was right by her side. Eventually, she would run up to say hello, tail wagging, letting them pet her on her head. She still wasn't ready for hugs from strangers or petting on the vigorous side, but she was getting used to other people. She would lie just outside the gym where I could see her out the window, and she could keep an eye on me as well.

As Clovis progressed with people, we knew it was time for a vet visit. Still unable to get her in our car and fearing that it would be too traumatic for her to go to an actual clinic, we called a mobile vet. We initially were going to use Beverly, our neighbor and vet, who had come by a few times to check on Clovis, but we needed someone who could treat Clovis at the house since we didn't want to take her in a car yet. The clinic that Beverly worked at was in a different town and we just couldn't get Clovis there without scaring her. At least three or four people highly recommended this particular mobile vet service, so we were anxious to make the appointment and get the news on Clovis' health. She looked healthy to us, other than that paw, but we had no idea if she had parasites, heartworms, or anything else. We had discovered that she had been spade at some point, so we assumed that she had also had her first round of shots, including rabies. This was one reason we had not worried about it to this point. But now it was time.

The Vet Gal and Guys from Southlake came to the house on March 2nd, and Clovis happily greeted them at the door. Excellent first step! Dr. Ashley Bellard and her assistant, Kathleen Elizondo, were fabulous with Clovis. Of course, Clovis took right to them as they gave her goodies of Cheese Whiz and peanut butter! After confirming that her left front paw was a birth defect and not trauma-related, they gave her the needed shots and the usual medications for flea and tick prevention. They scheduled a time to come back two days later to draw blood for the heartworm test as Clovis was a little shaken by the shots, and they didn't think they would be able to draw enough blood from her. With the help of some anti-anxiety medication, Clovis did get her blood draw on the 4th of March, and while it was quite an experience for her, she was fairly calm and so sweet during the procedure. This time, Dr. Lousia Sidwa came out, again, along with Kathy, to do the blood draw. She was just as nice and thorough as Dr. Bellard had been and Clovis, while scared due to the procedure, did beautifully. The Vet Gal and Guys were phenomenal and made the experience for Clovis as easy as possible. When they returned that second time to do the blood draw, Clovis happily greeted them at the door again, with no signs of wanting to withdraw or hide. What a long way this little girl had come!

After what seemed to be a very long three days wait for results, Clovis' tests for intestinal parasites came back negative. Great news! Unfortunately, the heartworm test did come back positive. "Wait! What? Lord, how can this be? I know You were caring for her and protecting her!" I thought to myself. I was having a difficult time believing it was positive. I just knew that she would be fine, that she would be as healthy as she could be. I also knew that God had kept her safe and protected her in so many ways.

I just didn't want to believe that He let this one thing "slip past" Him! As I talked with friends and clients about the diagnosis, I realized a couple of things: first, Clovis would now have a family and receive treatment for this. Otherwise, she would have died a very slow, painful, and lonely death outside on her own. I shudder to even think about that. Secondly, we live in a fallen world where accidents occur, people get sick, and bad things happen to everyone. No one is immune, no matter how spiritual and Christ-centered they may be. Yes, Clovis was ill and needed help. But many people are in the same position. I still believe that God protects and that He does heal today.

He most definitely is omniscient and omnipotent, having all knowledge and all power. He could take care of this, of course. But just as He uses struggles in our lives to teach us and make us stronger, with greater faith, He would use this to teach us once again. And He was using us in Clovis' life to help her, just as He was using her in ours. Lessons are learned through hardships and trials, not through perfect, problem-free lives.

Maybe this is just another way to show me His kindness and mercy so that I can then show the same to others in need. Still a bit anxious about it and sad that she had to go through the treatment, Randy and I decided to look at this from the positive side. Clovis was going to be OK because we had treated her to gain her trust. She would now be able to get better!

The vet explained that there were treatment options for the heartworms, and while Clovis didn't have any symptoms yet, we needed to get started as quickly as possible before more damage could be done to her lungs, heart, or other organs. Randy and I decided, along with the vet, to follow the "quick kill" method, which is costly and not that quick! It will be about a 4-month process but less likely to cause long-term damage than the slow kill method, which could take 18-24 months. Hopefully, this process will get started as soon as possible, although we now have one more hurdle to jump—getting Clovis into a car to take her to her treatments. "One step at a time, Stacie," I said to myself.

Finding out that Clovis would be required to go into the clinic for the heartworm treatment had us rethinking our plan. If the treatment could have been done at home, we would have stayed with the Vet Gal and Guys, who initially saw Clovis for her shots. However, since we would have to take her into the clinic, regardless of who treated her, we made the decision to use Beverly, our neighbor, friend, vet, and, yes, fellow runner. We know that she will be in good hands and are anxious to begin her treatments. Clovis has a lot of life yet to live! And I need my new sweet doggie to snuggle for as long as possible.

As I sit here now, thinking of Clovis and all she went through the last few years, all she experienced, and what she will go through during her treatment, I can't help but think of how God helped her. He led her to us and us to her. A dog that just a year ago ran from any sight of a human being, a dog that wouldn't look me in the eyes, a dog that wanted nothing to do with people in any way, shape, or form, now won't leave my side. It amazes me that now, Clovis wants to know where I am at all times.

She won't go out the gate without me. She is always checking to make sure I am with her. She follows me from room to room day in and day out, wanting to sit at my feet wherever I am. She is faithful to no end. It's as if she needs my confirmation before she does anything. Why this dramatic change? Because she now trusts me completely. She learned to trust Randy and me to take care of her, provide for her, and keep her safe.

Isn't this what the Lord wants from us? He wants us to trust Him completely and never leave His side, just as He promised never to leave ours. He desires for us to follow Him from room to room and sit at His feet, just as Mary sat at the feet of Jesus—just as Clovis sits at mine.

Maybe you have never been near to God or put your faith and trust in Jesus Christ. Or perhaps you have in the past, but for whatever reason, you have turned aside from His unfailing love. Randy, Clovis, and I want you to know that He is always waiting for you to come home.

He is waiting on you, and He is pursuing YOU, just as we pursued Clovis. One of Gateway's pastors, Jelani Lewis, once said, "Today, I encourage you—no matter how far away you think you've gone—to know that God is pursuing you with His love."

Just as we pursued Clovis with patience, kindness, and love, God is pursuing you for a relationship with Him, if you will just trust Him.

Epilogue

Clovis has now been with us for six full months! What a change we have seen in her and what joy she has brought to our home.

Clovis still follows me around everywhere. I can't get up to get a glass of water without her following me to see where I am going. Even now, she is lying at my feet, just wanting to be nearby. What a change from 1 year ago!

She is currently undergoing her heartworm treatment, and so far, she is doing wonderfully. For 60 days, she has to stay relatively still and calm, which is the hardest part for us. We wonder what she thinks about Mom and Dad not taking her out in the field to run anymore. She is being a real trooper, though.

Rocky, our "ferocious" cat, is now totally calm with Clovis. They walk up to each other, sniffing noses, without a ruffle or hiss whatsoever. Clovis can even run in from outside through the glass doors, bumping into Rocky as she goes, and Rocky sits there. I wish you knew how miraculous this truly is!

We still haven't managed to get Clovis into our car. Yes, we have tried everything. For some reason, she isn't ready, and that's OK. However, one day, I will have her in that car, driving to the lake, window rolled down with her head sticking out in the breeze! Fortunately, our friend and veterinarian, Beverly, is able to treat Clovis for her heartworms at our home. We are so very thankful for Beverly, who checks in on Clovis regularly and reassures me all the time that Clovis will, in fact, be fine.

As quiet as Clovis was for those three years, never barking at anyone, never approaching any other dog, she is now on high alert. While she is the sweetest dog, letting just about anyone pet her, if we are out in the yard and someone walks down the street, she acts as though she wants to go after them! If they have a dog with them? She barks ferociously, and I have to hold tight to her leash so that she won't chase them. Not really knowing what was going on, most people had said that while she was so quiet before, she was homeless. Now she has a home to protect. This is her house, and she is going to keep us safe. Still, it's a strange side of her to witness. Once she realizes that I think it's OK for someone to walk up, she will let them pet her, even rolling over on her back. But she wants to make sure that Mom and Dad approve of the visitor!

We did a DNA test on Clovis to find out what breed mix she was. It turns out she is 25% Rhodesian Ridgeback, 25% Catahoula Leopard Dog (a type of hound dog), 23% German Shepherd, and the rest a mix of American Pit Bull, Springer Spaniel, Bassett, and Great Pyrenees! We always suspected the first three as those were fairly obvious. I suppose way back in her lineage, you could find all the other breeds as well.

Clovis has settled in quite nicely, still sleeping on her comfy dog bed in our bedroom, never jumping up on our bed. While having her snuggle us in bed sounds wonderful, the kitties often sleep on our bed. Maybe Clovis is staying off our bed out of respect for the cats. Who knows! She has been amazing in the house. She doesn't climb on the furniture (only one sofa where we spread a blanket for her). She has never had an accident in the house, waiting patiently to go outside to potty, and she has never chewed up or destroyed anything in the house. She is as gentle as can be and easily trainable. She is learning simple commands and already knows many such as "lie down" or "wait."

My good friend and dog lover, Mindi, came by soon after Clovis had adjusted to being inside our home, bringing her a fun, pink toy to cuddle and squeak. Clovis loved it almost as much as Mindi loved the fact that I finally had a dog. Of course, I did have to ask her, "So, Mindi, I held up my end of the deal. When are you going to have a baby?" Her reply? "I'll start looking for a stray right away."

Often, I ask Randy, "Do you think Clovis misses being out on her own where she can roam the neighborhood and run through the woods?" Then we see her sleeping peacefully on our nice cool tile floor in this Texas heat, and we both answer with a resounding "NO!" If she does miss any part of her freedom from before, the love, warmth, and care she now feels are far greater than her desire to run freely. She has no intention of ever going back.

Randy and I would invite anyone who would love to see more pictures or videos of Clovis to follow her Facebook Page, entitled, "I Never Wanted a Dog." Additionally, if you are local and would ever want to visit, please reach out to us through her Facebook Page or email us at Ineverwantedadog@gmail.com. We would love to meet fellow dog lovers and those who have followed her story.

We thank you for your support and prayers for Clovis!

Stacie and Randy

About the Author

Stacie Sauber grew up in a family of eight in Bartlesville, Oklahoma. After marrying in 1987 and moving to the Dallas-Ft Worth area in 1990, she and her husband had four children and soon moved to Southlake, TX. In 2001, she and her husband divorced, and she remained and worked in Southlake until her last child graduated from high school in 2015. At that time, she met and married Randy Wolf, and they now work and reside in Grapevine, Texas.

Working as a personal trainer and raising four children wasn't an easy task, but one to which she was committed. Over those difficult years, the Lord taught her many things about her children, about herself, and most of all, about Him. The trials and difficulties—emotionally, financially, and even physically—pressed her to keep her eyes on her Provider and Redeemer. She thought she knew what love was. She thought she loved people. Little did she know that God was getting ready to teach her a much deeper love for His people, all by using a dog.

Stacie and Randy are members of Gateway Church in Southlake, TX, and they attribute much of what they know and have learned from their pastors at Gateway. As they continue to train and work with people to help them with their health and fitness, they also strive to help people with the health and fitness of their spiritual lives.